W9-BUZ-005

THE LIFE OF THE PEOPLE
IN BIBLICAL TIMES

THE
LIFE OF THE PEOPLE
IN BIBLICAL TIMES

BY

MAX RADIN

PHILADELPHIA
THE JEWISH PUBLICATION SOCIETY OF AMERICA
5708-1948

60

PRINTED IN THE UNITED STATES OF AMERICA
PRESS OF THE JEWISH PUBLICATION SOCIETY
PHILADELPHIA, PENNA.

CONTENTS

UXORI MEAE

HUNC LIBELLUM QUALISCUMQUE EST

QUEM EIUS OPE ET CONSILIO SCRIPSI

GRATO ANIMO ACCEPTUM REFERO

INTRODUCTION

BOOKS that describe the manners and customs of a bygone age constitute, it is well known, the driest and dustiest reading imaginable. And yet such books are indispensable if we desire to read the Bible intelligently. The men who wrote it wrote for people like themselves and they could be fairly certain that the words they used would conjure up pictures which did not differ from the reality they themselves had in mind. But when books survive as long as our biblical collection has survived, a certain discrepancy between intention and comprehension is inevitable. We continue to use the same words—we can scarcely do otherwise—but we must constantly bear in mind that the pictures these words now conjure up are quite unlike the pictures they called up for ancient writers. When we read the words "coat" or "shoe" or "bottle" or "table" in the Bible, we are not reading of the commodities which we know under those names but of things that resemble our articles only approximately. They fulfilled the same functions but they were quite different in structure and appearance. Even "house" and "window," "summer" and "winter," must be used with caution, although for ordinary purposes the resemblance is close enough. When the Bible is used solely for edification, that is, to furnish texts for homi-

lies, it really makes no difference whether we think of
Abraham as dressed in the garb of a wealthy American
merchant or in a coarse woolen cloak; whether David
is to be thought of in the steel panoply of a mediaeval
knight or in the Hussar uniform of a modern constitu-
tional monarch. But if we wish to read attentively
and if we regard the Bible as an imperishable record
of a literature and a civilization peculiarly interesting
to us, we must make the effort to reconstruct the concrete shell of the past as well as its essential spiritual
factors. Indeed, we shall be better able to apprehend
the latter if we attempt to vivify the background so
far as our imperfect information permits.

And our information is very imperfect indeed. Our
Bible, although we put it within the covers of a single
volume, is not a book but the remnants of a whole
literature. A great many things we should like to know
are simply not mentioned at all. We can resort to
archaeological remains—buildings, inscriptions, monuments—but there are relatively few of these, and while
the information derived from them is enormously
important, it does not fill all gaps by any manner of
means.

The term "Bible" is not Jewish but Christian, and
includes both the Old Testament and the New Testament. Plainly it is only the former that is meant
whenever the words "Bible" and "biblical" are used
in the following pages. The divisions of the Bible,
Pentateuch (Torah), Prophets (Nebiim), Writings

(Ketubim), and the individual books from Genesis to Chronicles were, by tradition as well as by modern criticism, written at different times. The most orthodox and conservative estimate places Malachi as well as Ezra and Nehemiah several centuries after the Return from Babylon in 538 B. C. E. The Bible therefore may be said to be all that has come down to us of the literature of the Jews from the earliest times up to about 300 B. C. E.

But books continued to be written after that date and some of those books have been preserved. One of them, indeed, we shall have to include in our survey, the book commonly called "Ecclesiasticus" or the "Wisdom of Jesus, the son of Sirach." It belongs to the "Apocrypha," the "Hidden Books," the non-canonical part of the Protestant Bible, although they form an integral part of the Catholic Bible. For many centuries it was known only in Greek, Syriac and Latin translations but the Hebrew text was rediscovered some thirty years ago by Dr. Solomon Schechter.

Apparently it was written about 200 B. C. E. by a Jew of Jerusalem named Jesus ben Sira. It was known to the Talmud and often referred to. We shall have occasion to speak of it frequently. It comes after the biblical period, but just after it. It gives us a peculiarly detailed picture of the spiritual and material life of post-exilic Judaism and is therefore a valuable source for the later part of the period which interests us.

It was long believed that the people who expressed
their soul in the Bible were determined beyond anything else by the nature of their religion.   Recently
we have been asked to believe that the God they worshipped was at first really not different in any way
from Chemosh, from Dagon and from Baal-Zebub,
and became different only gradually and in the minds
of an illuminated few. I venture to think this errone-
ous.   When certain wandering tribes accepted the
covenant of the Lord—somewhere in the desert across
the Jordan and at some time before the twelfth century B. C. E.—they were swept with an enthusiastic
sense of becoming the special people of their God.
And He was a very different God from others. That
He was the bestower of good upon those whom He
loved, that He was the Lord of the Universe, would
have been no new thing. Just so that strange figure,
the Pharaoh Akhn-aton, addressed his new symbol of
the Divine Principle. But the God of the Covenant
called Himself by a name quite new in the titularies of
gods. He was a God of compassion. His most accepted
sacrifice was a broken and a contrite heart.

It was a new idea in that part of the world. We may
be sure it was only imperfectly understood, and that
it was not until much later that even the more obvious
applications were made. But even the vague presence
of this idea changed the aspect of life.

Israel, triumphant in Palestine, more than once tried
to make of their covenant God the lord of the land,

a Baal of Baalim. The attempt was never quite successful. The recollection of the mighty man who taught them at the foot of Sinai, remained as a constant stimulus to prophet after prophet to recall the people to a sense of the special character of their divine protector. That their Lord was highly personal was of course true. That much of their concept of Him reflected their rude lives and their own intense spirit is equally true. Nor did His existence seem at first to negate the existence of other gods for other peoples. But He was a different God from those others. He did not ask what they did. He showed Himself in no form that could be ascribed to them. He held His people in a mystic espousal as no other did.

I think the life of the biblical people would have been quite different had their God been, as the half savage Jephthah thought, merely the Israelitish counterpart of Chemosh. Their history might have run about the same course till the Exile. Their speech, their manners, their clothes, their appearance, their habits of daily life, would have been very nearly the same. But their attitude toward life would have been different and this attitude could not help having its direct and concrete expression.

Yet in the following pages it is not the spirit that made them different but the environment that made them like their neighbors, that will chiefly engage our attention. To depict a spirit is too large a task. Those who would understand this spirit can do so more immediately and more fully than by studying any book on manners and customs. They can read the Bible.

CHAPTER I

THE TIME AND THE PEOPLE

THERE are several preliminary matters that must be understood before we can set to our proper task—the examination and depiction of the life of the people in biblical times. In the first place we must be sure of our subject. What were biblical times and who were the people? Framed this way, the questions seem simple and fundamental enough, but when we look at the matter more closely they are not so easy to answer.

"Biblical times" is a very vague term. For our present purposes we shall understand by it the period during which the Bible was written. That covers a considerable time. Between the writing of the oldest passage in the Bible and the latest, more than a thousand years elapsed. Manners and customs change notably in such a stretch of time. We can realize how much, if we compare the England of Eadwaerd, King of Wessex, who reigned in 924, with the England of King George V of 1924. And if that is so in the case of England, it is likely to have been so during a similar period in Palestine. For we must not delude ourselves by such phrases as the "unchanging East" into believing that any group of men anywhere really does not change. There are many things about them that, as a matter of fact, change very slightly. Just what these things are depends upon the people. It often happens that a characteristic which we know well and which has varied greatly in Western Europe has scarcely changed at all, or has not changed in the same way, in the Orient. That is what the phrase means, if it means anything.

Besides, so far as biblical times are concerned, the changes involved were not only those that the mere lapse of years brings, but they were further the changes that are inevitable when a nomad horde invades and gradually settles a cultivated region and becomes, first a military and aggressive kingdom with all the appurtenances of civilization, and finally a highly organized and sophisticated community governed by a priestly caste. Changes so profound in social structure would necessitate a separate treatment for the life of each distinct epoch. Since that is impossible in the space of a small book, we shall have to represent on a single canvas what really was a succession of pictures. It will have very much the effect of ancient bas-reliefs or of Chinese paintings, in which one plane is superimposed upon another, and by a readily accepted convention, we profess to see depth where we have only surfaces.

In most cases, accordingly, it will be remembered that the details of life here mentioned side by side may be derived from stories or accounts separated in time by several hundred years. Occasionally the differences caused by time will be alluded to, but that will not always be possible.

Biblical times, then, cover roughly the period between 1200 B. C. E. and 200 B. C. E. and concern themselves with the fortunes of the people who in that millennium inhabited Palestine. And just what we mean by Palestine we shall, I trust, fully discover in the next chapter.

However, we cannot deal with all the people in this country. We are really concerned only with those whose literature the Bible is. To be sure, we shall have to speak of their neighbors, but the latter are not the people whose life is mentioned in the title of this book. That people is the Jews.

The Jews are spoken of as a part of the Semitic race. If we mean by that a people speaking a Semitic language, the statement is literally true, and that is the only significance modern anthropologists will permit us to give to the phrase "Semitic race." If we mean, by calling them Semites, to assert that they had exactly the same physical inheritance as the Mesopotamians, the Syrians or the Arabs of their day, and as the corresponding nations have who bear those names today, the statement is manifestly untrue. The Jews in Palestine or Canaan were to a considerable extent physically the kin of other Canaanites, and these Canaanites in the main had resided in the country long before the first Semitic-speaking tribe filtered in from the desert. And many generations before the

Bible reached its present form, men of widely varying physical origin had in one way or another become amalgamated with the Canaanite Jews. It is perfectly proper to call them Semites if we mean language and, to a large extent, culture. It does not really help us to give them that name, if we mean anything more.

And it is important to keep that fact in mind because the terms "race" and "Semite" have been handled quite freely and without much conscience or reflection by the writers of the early nineteenth century and by many men of later times who ought to have known better. That would be no great matter if these same terms had not been made pretexts for the rousing of national and religious hatreds and for gratifying the evil lusts of the agitators who use them. The less frequently they are used, the better and less colored our conception of the time will be.

In 1200 B. C. E. this people already had a past. Their traditions knew of an ancient migration from Mesopotamia and a more recent one from Egypt, where they or some of them had been serfs—or perhaps a subjugated people compelled to pay heavy tribute in labor and in produce for the right to occupy a portion of the land. At any rate they were not primitive and had been in intimate contact with two great centers of civilization for a long while. Rude in a sense they still were—for their traditions represent them as having relapsed into nomad life after an experience as a settled people. And they had accepted a religion, which was preached with a mystical fervor and an ethical force that made it very attractive, but which had grown up in a small and isolated group. This religion was fundamentally opposed to cities and the customs of cities and formed therefore a real check upon the rate at which the Jews absorbed the ancient material culture of Canaan. Besides, it gave a direction to their social and personal development that must at no stage be left out of account.

The use of a correct national designation for the people has certain difficulties. They may be called Hebrews, Israelites or Jews. These terms have unfortunately assumed a certain emotional coloring in recent times and the use of the term Hebrew or Israelite is often taken to be a euphemism—an attempt to avoid the word Jew with its associations of ghetto and pogrom. The terms are not really identical, so that accurate historians will no doubt resent their being confused.

There is, after all, no special mystery about it. Hebrew is the name properly applied to the nomad Semites who began to invade Canaan about 1400 B. C. E. and who included among their numbers the ancestors of the biblical Jews. But they also included Midianites, Amalekites, Moabites, Ammonites, Edomites—all bitter enemies of the Jews, however close their kinship. They do not seem to have included the Phoenicians who represent one of the first and in a sense the most successful wave of the Semitic invasion.

And they may have included the Ishmaelites although these men of the desert did not join the invaders except as individuals.

Israelites, again, are the tribes—twelve by tradition —who under the hegemony of one of them—Manasseh, Benjamin, Judah and Ephraim in that historical order —organized a kingdom, that is a state of greater or less stability and finally of considerable power under the dynasty of Jehu. This state was completely and deliberately destroyed in 720 B. C. E. by the Assyrians. Properly, therefore, one should not speak of Israelites after that date, unless the pitifully dwindling Samaritans correctly claim that designation.

The Jews again are so often contrasted with the Israelites in the Bible that it seems almost as though their association with Israel was temporary and that in the time of Jeroboam I, Judah merely resumed its former independence when it lost its supremacy. However that may be, they were surely only one of the tribes that entered into the state organization of David and Solomon and it is from them, not from Israel as a whole, that the modern Jews are descended.

So we may say that the broadest term is Hebrew, which includes Israelite and many others; that the next broadest is Israelite, which includes the Jews and others.

Yet it is an obvious fact that all those "others" have disappeared as conscious units, and that the Jews still remain as such. They are therefore the sole heirs of Hebrew and Israelite as well as of their more immediate ancestor, Judah the son of Jacob. In their traditions, from the time of their first separate emergence to the present day, they have claimed that inheritance and it seems pedantic to refuse it to them.

Accordingly in the following pages we shall find Hebrew, Israelite or Jew used indiscriminately for the "people of biblical times," and those who know will make their own corrections.

If we could conjecture by what name they would have liked to be called, it would probably have been "the people of the Lord." They thought the bond that united them and distinguished them from others to be a religious bond and not one of blood. And, as a matter of fact, they were almost surely right in that respect. Kenite or Hittite might be a believer and thus a member of the community, however remote his blood affiliation was; but Amalekite and Moabite, undoubted brethren in blood, were not members.

In Scotland in the early days of Protestantism, earnest adherents of the new faith bound themselves by a Solemn League and Covenant to fight for the Congregation of the Lord against the Congregation of Satan. The next century is full of accounts of the bitter and bloody way in which the Covenanters maintained and defended their faith. In the same way, when somewhere in the Syrian desert certain nomad tribes embraced with enthusiasm the strange and new worship of Sinai, they entered into what seemed to them a

Solemn Covenant. As men of that Covenant, they invaded and conquered the better part of Palestine. In many ways—in intensity, in steadfastness, in martial ardor—they greatly resembled those Covenanters who many centuries later and so far away, consciously formed themselves upon the ancient model. We may call this more ancient Congregation of the Lord by that same name of Covenanters if only to borrow the suggestion of violent zeal conveyed by the word.

The people of biblical times were, as a mass, a people of settled homes and peaceable pursuits, but the covenanting leaven never died out in them, and bubbled up from time to time in prophet or in warrior, or in men who were both. The great literature whose fragments we call the Bible, if it is the record of a single spirit, is, in effect, a "Book of the Covenant" in the largest sense we can give to that term.

CHAPTER II

THE LAND

WHEN we speak of a country, we are primarily concerned with the inhabitants, those who actually live in it, have lived in it, or will live in it. It needs no special argumentation to prove that the interest of Palestine for us lies in the fact that it formerly was the home of the Jews. But it is a truism among historians that a people are, at least in part, what the country they live in makes them. Its position on the surface of the earth, its physical features, its distribution of land and water, its rocks and its soil and the things dug therefrom or planted therein, the winds that blow over it—all these are not merely useful bits of general information, they are vitally necessary, if we wish to understand what manner of men dwelt in the country, what they were able to accomplish and what things were denied to them.

Now, it is likely that the first impression of Palestine will be the contrast between the climate of Palestine and the climate of our own country. Palestine is a sub-tropical country. That means, for practical purposes, that Palestine is somewhat hotter than, let us say, New York, but it is not anything like so hot as a really tropical country, Central Africa, for instance, or Southern India. There are indeed parts of Palestine

—the Jordan Valley, for example, where the river enters the Dead Sea—which in climate, in fauna and flora, are very much like tropical regions; but in the main Palestine has a climate much resembling that of our Southern States. And if it is hotter than New York, it is quite without the bewildering and tremendous changes in climate that make New York and other cities familiar to us so full of surprises to strangers.

And the seasons, too, are different. The succession of spring, summer, autumn and winter exists to be sure, but it does not quite mean for Palestine what it means for us. Spring and summer and autumn are merely names for different kinds of harvests, and all together they make up the "dry" season, the "fine weather," when the sun is pretty certain to shine constantly and rain is so rare that its occurrence savors of the miraculous. This lasts for nearly six months, from April to October. The other six months which make up the "winter," are the "wet" season. This does not mean that it will rain every day, but it does mean that it may rain any day and that in the early part of the "winter" a series of light showers is likely to occur and in the latter part a series of heavier showers, the "former" and the "latter" rain, so often mentioned in the Bible.

Many Americans will recognize seasons like these at once. Something very like this prevails on the Western coast of the United States, and particularly in California. Indeed the similarity between the physi-

cal conditions of Southern California and those of
Palestine is so great that those who wish to prepare
themselves for the rehabilitation of Palestine find
California an extraordinarily favorable place in which
to gain the necessary skill and experience.

The sowing and plowing time is in the early autumn
and not in "spring," although a supplemental sowing
takes place at the end of "winter." Then during the
"summer," men harvested first the grain, then the
fruit and finally the grapes. That is not at all the image
ordinarily presented to our mind when we read the
words of God's promise to Noah that "seed-time and
harvest" shall not cease, and men's lives were very
differently ordered when the seasons were divided
after this fashion.

Palestine is not only a sub-tropical country, that is,
generally hotter than the regions we are accustomed
to, but in the parts that are most associated with the
Jews it is poorly watered. It is not arid. We must not
imagine that any part of Palestine proper, except in
the most southerly section, presents anything like the
appearance of a desert. Nor is the lack of water serious
enough to constitute a real detriment to the physical
well-being of the inhabitants. But there is no such
plenty as that which we know. The lavish use of
water that characterizes American life is certainly not
feasible in Palestine. Rain is infrequent except at
certain definite times of the year, a fact that must
give ordinary life an aspect quite different from that

of the United States. The water supply must be carefully husbanded and wisely distributed. It will admit
of neither waste nor profusion.

Whether the water supply, for purposes of human
life, can or can not be improved, the effect on the land
of the condition just described is the relative absence
of trees, especially large ones. Trees were more or less
plentiful in the north, although even here much less
numerous than in the United States. But in Judea
and the section just north of it, trees of any kind are
a rarity. It is this that made trees an object of venera-
tion and worship to the heathen Palestinian, a fact to
which the Bible amply testifies. When we think of an
open countryside, we think of it as covered with a
wealth of trunks and foliage. Nothing of this sort
must be associated with a Palestinian landscape.

But if large trees are scarce, there is an abundant
growth of other things. On the plains and some of the
hillsides, the meadows are alive with flowers, and the
variety is as bewildering as the display is dazzling.
There are few more gorgeous spectacles on the face
of the earth—if sober travellers are to be credited—
than the spring investiture of the plains of Sharon.
And even where the hues are less alluring, there is no
lack of green shrubbery, bearing constant witness to
the readiness of the soil to do its part, if man will do
his.

I have mentioned these two details first because
they seem to me of great significance. They are, to

be sure, not the first things that suggest themselves
when we hear the phrase, the "Geography of Palestine." But they are such striking facts, such generally
pervading facts, that they ought to be made to color
any thoughts that we may have about the characteristics of the country, and for that reason cannot
be mentioned too soon or dwelt on too insistently.

What the term geography does suggest is a map,
and a map, I am afraid, is likely to arouse recollec-
tions that are not altogether happy. The study of
maps is not classed among the commonest diversions
even by educated people. Perhaps that is due to re-
membrances of childhood struggles with the geography
lesson, often the least popular and least inspiring part
of the school course. What made the geography lesson distasteful was the tax it laid on our memories,
the burden it imposed of keeping in mind unrelated
facts about countries in which we had no immediate
or pressing interest.

Most people measurably familiar with the map of
the world find themselves associating any given country with a definite shape. So Italy is a boot; Scandi-
navia looks like a leaping beast of prey; Greece is
principally connected with the three fingers of the
Peloponnesus. The map of Palestine has no such easily remembered form. Any public school child in
America will doubtless find a general resemblance between the map of Palestine and the map of the State
of New Hampshire. It is a four-sided, perhaps five-

sided, figure, of which one side tilts northeast, and of
which the upper part is markedly narrower than the
lower. Just what its boundaries are, is not easy to
determine. In what follows we shall sedulously avoid
controversies by confining ourselves to what is practically undisputed.

There is one boundary of Palestine that cannot
readily be disputed and that is the western boundary,
the Mediterranean Sea. The southern coast of Asia
Minor and the northern coast of Egypt and Sinai
make almost right angles with a line running north
and south and marking the eastern limit of the Mediterranean. One fourth of this line is the western
boundary of Palestine. At the very extreme south of
it is the little village of Rapha, now an important
station on the railroad that made Allenby's campaign
possible. We shall have occasion to come back to
Rapha and shall therefore do well to keep it in mind.
It is the southwesterly point of the boundaries of
Palestine.

The question is, how much of the coastline constitutes this western boundary of Palestine. Between
the ancient Sidon and Tyre we come to the mouth of
a river. It is called the Nahr-el-Khasimiyeh, and for
part of its course at least it is also called the Litani,
a name that perpetuates its ancient designation, the
Leontes. That Palestine, on its western border, goes
as far as this, will not be seriously gainsaid, and for
the present, we shall rest content with that.

This coast, from Rapha to the Khasimiyeh, as can be seen by a glance at the map, is a very different thing from the eastern coast line of the United States. The line is practically straight until we come to Haifa, the bay of Akko or Acre, the first step in the "Syrian Stair." The straight shore line is, of course, a geographic fact of the first importance. It means with the exception noted, that there are no harbors, and how vital such a lack is need scarcely be insisted upon. It is true that the absence of harbors can be partially overcome by the erection of artificial moles and breakwaters. Tyre, without a harbor except for such contrivances, managed to achieve a commercial supremacy of which the echoes have not died away in four thousand years. But that was under conditions that were radically different from those of the present day. Breakwaters and dikes will help, but they will not permit the creation of ports that can seriously compete with those that have good natural harbors in the vicinity.

As has been suggested, the northern boundary is a matter of spirited debate. Accepting the Khasimiyeh as that boundary, and it is a deep and impressive stream for that region, we may follow it till it abruptly bends to the north. Taking a line from there' due east, we shall have a northern boundary that will be practically unchallenged.

How far east, is something that is not merely difficult, but nothing short of impossible to decide. The eastern boundary is certainly not the Jordan. It may be true that in the Bible, the East-Jordan territory is treated as something different, something exceptional. But it is equally true that it would be hard to find a time when some part of the Trans-Jordan territory was not controlled by those who dominated in the West-Jordan land.

Once we cross the Jordan there is no stopping. We may stop at this or that parallel of longitude, but parallels of longitude are less formidable barriers than they seem to be on the map. Somewhere in what is now a desert ran the eastern boundary of "Palestine," though we cannot determine it precisely. The present Hedjaz Railroad, which follows the old Mohammedan pilgrim route, will be a convenient stopping point.

This, then, is what I shall mean when I speak of Palestine, to wit, the country from Rapha on the Mediterranean north to the mouth of the Nahr-el-Khasimiyeh; thence due east to near the Hedjaz Railroad; from there south to a point at or near Maan; from there southwest to the Gulf of Akabah and again northwest back to Rapha. This makes a five-sided figure, of which the longest side is about 180 or 200 miles and the shortest side cannot be more than 60. We may say that roughly it equals Massachusetts and Connecticut combined.

Now what sort of land is there in this irregular pentagon? It divides itself quite naturally into a number of longitudinal strips. Beginning again at Rapha, and following the coast, there is the Maritime Plain. We have first the ancient Philistia, so long a thorn in the side of Israel and Judah, which continues into the Plains of Sharon, and after being interrupted by Mt. Carmel, is continued into Phoenicia.

This maritime plain is of remarkable fertility. Many of the modern Jewish colonies are located here. Past history and present promise unite in making it one of the regions of Palestine that must engage our immediate and close attention. The richness of Sharon has already been referred to. In ancient times this plain was notable not merely for the intrinsic value of the soil, but chiefly as the great route from the North into Egypt. The hosts of forgotten nations rolled along it to and from the granary of the Nile, and kept so close to the shore that to many of them the very existence of such cities as Jerusalem may well have been unknown. The southern portion of it, seized by Cretan pirates, became under the Philistines the domain of a confederation of cities which achieved little of permanent value but are remembered chiefly for having given Palestine its name, and for having afforded Israel that discipline of struggle and adversity from which alone significant nations arise.

North of Mt. Carmel was the region occupied by the earliest Semitic invasion of Canaan, that of the Phoenicians. The great group of Phoenician cities performed such notable functions in the spread of civilized arts that the petty little villages which alone recall

the glories of Tyre and Sidon are melancholy remind-
ers of the most commonplace of historical truisms.
This section of the Maritime Plain was, however, never
a part of Jewish or Israelitish dominion.

The Maritime Plain is cut in two by Mt. Carmel,
which juts into the sea from the highlands of Samaria
to the Bay of Haifa. That ancient river, the River
Kishon, flows into the bay, past Mt. Carmel, and thus
gives this particular point a double association for
Jews. And just north of Mt. Carmel, the great plain
of the Sea is continued into the broad valley of Esdraelon, straight to the Jordan. All that can be said of
the fertility and economic importance of the coast
plain can be repeated and emphasized of Esdraelon.
On that point we are not reduced to conjecture or even
to the recollection of past achievement. Esdraelon,
even in the last years of the Turkish rule, was produc-
ing great quantities of wheat as well as fruits and
vegetables.

The second of the longitudinal strips which constitute Palestine consists of a series of low limestone hills.
In the south they form the Shephela, in which the date
and olive flourish and in which the coarser forms of
grain will readily thrive. North of Samaria, these hills
are interrupted by the Plain of Esdraelon and do not
form so recognizable a feature of the land.

It is the next strip, "the Western Mountain Range,"
that has seen the major part of Jewish history. And
it is precisely the most forbidding and least fertile

section, the mountains of Judea, with which our holiest memories are associated. The Jews were mountaineers, Highlanders. The bare limestone of their native soil offered them but a niggardly subsistence. It put no obstacle in the way of that vastly higher development to which alone the Jews owe their survival and their national individuality. Among its hills stands the symbol and crown of their greatness, the Holy City of Jerusalem. Judea is a stony plateau, wholly without running water, but none the less capable of a certain cultivation, principally of olive and barley. The pasturing of flocks was in ancient times the most important occupation. The plateau of Judea, after a slight depression, is almost continuous with the highlands of Samaria, the Mount of Ephraim of the Bible. Here, however, a number of fertile valleys give the country a wholly different aspect. One of these contains both Shechem and Samaria, the capitals of Israel.

When we cross Esdraelon again to enter the highlands of Galilee, it is in a wholly different region that we find ourselves. Here are hills covered with thick shrubbery which might well be trees. Are not the cedars of Lebanon in sight? These hills of Galilee, as well as the valleys below them, were once thickly populated. Their fertility is apparent from the fact that even gross neglect has not impaired their productivity.

To the east, the hills of Galilee, of Samaria, and of Judea fall rapidly into the Jordan Valley, which has been denominated "the deepest trench on the surface of the earth." Beginning far north on the slopes of Mt. Hermon, the head-waters of the Jordan gather into sizable streams, and at the site of the ancient Dan already form a river to be reckoned with. It flows at very nearly the level of the sea, till we reach Lake Huleh, the smallest and most northerly of the three lakes through which the Jordan runs. Then the bed sinks rapidly, as the temperature of the valley rises, until at about the northern half of Esdraelon, we reach the sea of Gennesaret, 680 feet below the level of the sea, a warm and fertile valley.

When the Jordan leaves Gennesaret it descends deeper and deeper through the cleft called the Ghor, to the Dead Sea, nearly 1300 feet below the surface of the sea. Of this body of water, one of the most famous of natural phenomena, it is unnecessary to say much. In spite of its fame—for it has excited the interest and curiosity of strangers for much more than three thousand years—sections of the shore are only slightly known.

Most of the detailed historical associations of the Jews are with the West-Jordan land. But as far as sheer richness of soil is concerned, the West-Jordan territory must yield to that across the Jordan, into which neglect and maladministration have allowed the desert to creep almost to the Jordan valley. Beginning

at Mt. Hermon—the Anti-Lebanon—we come to the
highlands of Iturea, famous in Roman times for the
sturdy soldiers that it bred. Below Iturea, is Bashan,
equally famous for its forests of oaks and its magnificent cattle. Very few of the oaks are left. The plains
are almost entirely devoid of trees. But there is everywhere unmistakable proof that this is due to man's
improvidence.

Iturea and Bashan as well as Golan, right at the
Jordan, form part of the region which in its entirety
is called the Hauran. The southern boundary of the
Hauran is at the River Yarmuk, a rapid and perennial
river just below Gennesaret. The soil of the whole
Hauran is of volcanic origin, and as in all such cases,
of remarkable fertility. The wheat of the Hauran in
variety and quality is famous throughout the East.
It was one of the granaries of Syria.

Further than that, the climate of the Hauran with
its even moderate days and cool nights, is of singular
amenity. In Greek and Roman times, the region just
below the Yarmuk, which is of much the same character as the Hauran itself, was the seat of the city-federa-
tion known as the Decapolis. Magnificent ruins attest
its past prosperity.

Between the Yarmuk and the vigorous stream of
the Jabbok, forty miles further south, at about the
line of Samaria, lies Gilead. Gilead is a series of limestone hills. Its climate is like that of the Hauran,
fresh and even, and its fertility almost as exuberant.

In marked contrast with most of western Palestine, trees are fairly numerous, and the country is lined with streams.

Below the Jabbok begin the ancient lands of Israel's kinsmen and hereditary enemies, Ammon and Moab. This is a high wind-swept plateau of gray limestone, bearing wheat and abundant pasture. Though it seems difficult to associate severe winters with Palestine, the winters of Moab are said to be somewhat too rigorous.

The country to the south of the Dead Sea is little known. It has rarely been visited because of the insecurity of the trip, although it contains such famous ruins as those of Petra. There can be no doubt, however, that here we are in a real desert country.

As we swing west again—or rather northwest—we reach Rapha over the Arabah, the ancient Negeb or "Parched Land." The country is almost waterless, except that in the short rainy season the dry and deep gullies, still called Wadis, suddenly swell into torrents, and waste their priceless moisture in the thirsty soil. This sudden filling of the gullies, dry for the greater part of the year, gives life to the exultant simile of the *Shir ha-Ma'alot*, that Song of Ascents (Psalm 126), sung in countless Jewish homes on Friday evening. "Turn again our captivity, Oh Lord, like the streams in the Negeb." We can readily imagine with what a sense of an annual miracle this rapid change from arid waste to abundance impressed the ancient dwellers.

In a country like this, so watered, so warmed, so cultivated, the Bible was written, and all its incidents are framed against this background. Whatever the Israelites or Hebrews were when they entered Palestine—and they were a nation before they crossed the Jordan—they grew to maturity here, and as we shall have abundant occasion to see, the country played a powerful part in making them. They thought it was a land flowing "with milk and honey", and they could scarcely know that there are many parts of the world much more productive and of much greater natural riches above and below the surface. But if we keep in mind what has been stated here, we shall also realize that it is not a poor and desolate little corner of the earth, but an extraordinary land of great variety within its small compass and with some features that are quite unique. It bred a "peculiar" people and their difference from their neighbors was to some extent due to their land.

CHAPTER III

THE HOUSEHOLD AND ITS MEMBERS

A MODERN nation is a group of individual citizens. It is of course quite true that they are far from being such separate and independent persons as they often think themselves, and one of the most prominent facts about them is the readiness with which they enter into associations of all kinds—churches, societies, fraternal organizations, trade unions and the like. Indeed, it often seems that they are as much born into such associations as they are into the group of which the tie is peculiarly birth—that of the family. The bonds made by the common interest of all these societies and groups are very real and, as we know, powerfully affect all our thinking and acting.

Yet in spite of these groupings and the bonds they create, we maintain in theory that we are individuals, that no group, except possibly the family, has a hold on us that we cannot shake off at will so that we can rearrange our social relations as we choose. And even in the family we like to think of the bonds as only partially obligatory. In modern times men have certainly relaxed these bonds in a number of ways—have narrowed their operation—and while it is still morally reprehensible to refuse to admit that family ties exist, such refusal is possible.

Now an ancient people was not so constituted either in practice or in theory. The state, whether it took the form of a nomad horde—that is, either a loose confederation of clans, or a single large clan—or a settled agricultural community or an aggressive military kingdom, was based not on the individual, but on the family. It was an aggregation of families, not of single persons. Anyone who for one reason or another was not a member of some family group was not a citizen of the community. The only conceivable exception was the last survivor of any family group which had, as a group, been a member of the state.

What was the family? It consisted of one man— the master or *ba'al*, or father, *ab*, and those who in some way were dependent upon him. The proof of that dependence was generally that they lived in his house, or, if we imagine him to be a wealthy landowner, in one of the several houses that formed a single large estate. The dependents were his wife or wives, his children, his slaves and his clients, the latter being generally foreigners who were temporarily or permanently residents of the country. Among the Romans the dependence of all the members of the household on the father never ceased as long as he lived, unless he voluntarily surrendered his rights or forfeited them as a penalty. This was not so among the Hebrews. It might happen frequently that an adult male would leave his father's house and found one himself and apparently he could not be prevented from doing that if he chose to.

First of all, then, a family consisted of the *ba'al ha-bayit* or *ab* and his women-folk. That a man might be a bachelor, that is, live quite alone without a wife, was practically inconceivable. Certainly we hear of no such case. As a matter of fact, there is no word for bachelor, or unmarried adult man, in biblical Hebrew. The nearest word to it, *'elem*, or marriage-able young man, denoted a very young man indeed, such as the youthful David was when he first caught the attention of Saul. Or it is the word *bahur*, one of those "choice young men and goodly" who were doing their military service about some renowned captain and only waiting for temporary repose from such activities to take wives or receive them as prizes for their efforts.

The wife, or mother, *ishah*, *em*, held an important position in the household. She had a claim to rever-ence equal to that of the father. The king himself bows down to his mother and seats her at his right hand, as the gorgeous Solomon did to Bathsheba. As far as her children are concerned, she gives commands on equal terms with her husband. It is only the "fool-ish man," the type of arrogant perversity, who dis-obeys his mother, say the words of the wise. And as to offering either mother or father violence in word or deed, by curse or by blow, the offense was capital. "He shall surely be put to death." The very "making light" of father or of mother was classed with idolatry and murder. Killing of a parent—actual parricide—was too unthinkable even to be mentioned in the law as a crime. Such a thing might and did happen only to wicked heathen kings bowing down in the house of their gods, as when Adrammelech and Sharezer slew Sennacherib at his prayers.

Further, whenever in precepts or in Psalms or Proverbs filial devotion is mentioned, father and mother are regularly made equal, as is done in the Fifth Commandment. The duty to the one was no greater and no less than to the other. And since filial devotion is the foundation virtue of ancient society, this gives the mother a very high and important place in the structure of that society.

Of course this is quite what we should expect in either the ancient or the modern world. It was true of Athens, where women were practically locked up for most of their adult lives, as they are in many parts of the modern Orient. The Jewish matron was not locked up and she went about freely when she chose, but it was expected of her that she would so choose but rarely. Indeed, we should be inclined to assert that a great deal was expected of her. At the end of our book of Proverbs there is an acrostic psalm which may be called the Song of the Woman of Valor, the *Eshet Hayil*. From it we learn what the ideal woman did or was supposed to do. She had complete charge of the preparation and distribution of food in the household. She directed the household arts, the spinning and weaving, and herself took a large part in them. She was the chief steward. She examined the merchandise to be bought and even had the decision, or at any rate gave valuable advice, in purchase of landed estate. Again, she sold the surplus gear of the house and bargained with the foreign traders. As far as the field work was concerned, she confined her activities to garden and vineyard and apparently left the plowing and threshing and gleaning to the men. She apportioned and supervised the labor of the female slaves, but not of the male slaves. And, finally, she was the almoner of the household. She distributed the charitable doles, which were an essential part of the duties of an honorable family.

It is even stated that she "riseth also while it is yet night," which seems a little unreasonable in addition to so much else, but we hasten to note that scholars are not quite sure that this is the meaning of the biblical expression—so there is after all no certain biblical warrant that discomfort is in itself a mark of virtue in man or woman.

Still the day described is a pretty full one, and gives the matron a predominating position in the household economy. It is extraordinary that the work of the kitchen is not mentioned, and it may be only an inadvertence, for both Rebekah and Tamar prepared and dressed meats. And yet on the whole most of the instances of preparing and serving food are told of men. Some centuries later the preparation and serving of food were very distinctly women's work, under male supervision, to be sure. Among Greeks and Romans it had long been so, and we must conjecture that the disinclination of the Jews to part with what was perhaps an ancient masculine monopoly was the close association among them of ritual with food.

The matron, then, was a hardworking person; but it is pleasant to remember that her toil was duly appreciated. "Her children arise up and call her blessed: her husband also and he praiseth her." She seems at all times to have been treated with deference by her husband. This is particularly noteworthy in a polygamous society. As late as the fourth century C. E. the Jews were charged with pampering their wives, and that by St. Jerome, a Roman and a Christian! There is no instance in the Bible of brutal treatment of a wife by a husband, and women appear as prophetesses, as queens, as poets, as wise persons whose counsels would prevail in war. If they appear also as false prophetesses, as wicked and bloody rulers, as evil counsellors, they may claim even this fact as a tribute to their power and influence.

And yet it would be quite far-fetched to assert that there was anything like sex-equality, or even marital equality, in ancient Israel. The wife was distinctly the inferior. Her adultery was punishable with death. Her husband was her master, *ba'al;* she addressed him as "My lord." There is no evidence that she had control of any property, except as her husband's agent and steward. She might be divorced at will by a simple "bill of divorcement." To be sure, there were certain restrictions upon divorce, but not many, and she could not under any circumstances divorce her husband. She was, however, fairly secure if she had a male child. Her husband could not cast her off without the child to whose service and reverence she had an equal claim with him. Such a case as that of Abraham and Hagar was treated by the legends as extremely exceptional and not very creditable even in the "Friend of God." One is inclined to say in such cases that later men would not have thought of regulating their lives altogether by patriarchal examples. What happened before the Law was given on Sinai was one thing. Later generations were bound to obey the Law. We can therefore understand the peculiar desolation of the childless wife and the utter despair of the cry, "Give me children or I die." Few childless women could count on an indulgent husband such as Elkanah and even his indulgence did not save his favorite from the taunts of the "adversary," the second and the fruitful wife.

If the woman was a widow, to be sure, she had both property and, one may suppose, independent control of it. The handmaid who is her mistress' heir, indicates both facts. But unless she had male kinsmen willing and able to protect her, she was clearly in a pitiful state, since the desolation and helplessness of a widow are proverbial expressions throughout the Bible. That must be due to her incapacity to appear in any public proceedings. In a way, therefore, widows and orphans were wards of the people as a whole, and a man's character was tested by his conduct toward these helpless members of the community.

If there were several wives, they were probably settled in different houses. There is scarcely any doubt that monogamy was the rule. The chief reason for this fact seems to be the poverty of the people as a whole. It is quite clear, however, that there was nothing reprehensible in plurality of wives. It was a proof of wealth and power and was therefore peculiarly a means of ostentation, from the king downward. Two wives were not uncommon in the case of a man of moderate means. In fact when more than one wife is mentioned, it is generally implied that there were two. Curiously enough, in later law they might not be sisters, in spite of the example of Leah and Rachel. But it is noteworthy that Noah, Abraham and Isaac have each only one wife and the coupling of "father and mother" in so many proverbs and laws points to a monogamous household. The inevitable jealousies of two mistresses of a house had no slight influence in favor of monogamy. The two wives of Jacob and of Elkanah, the story of Hagar and Sarah, show how prominent a part in popular imagination was played by this unpleasant side of large establishments. The word translated in the Bible as "second wife" means literally "adversary."

The children, as long as they remained in the house, were under the complete control of their parents. Unfilial or undutiful conduct was, as has been said, not merely a moral offense, it was a capital crime. The sons labored in the fields and the daughters assisted their mother in the duties described above. On the whole their position in the household was scarcely different from that of indulged slaves.

The sons left the household and the control of their father when they felt competent to establish and support a house by their own efforts. This did not always or even commonly take place at marriage, for they were married quite young, just upon attaining puberty, or soon after, and the daughter-in-law took her place in the household with her husband's sisters. But when the young man was full grown, it seems to have been a common practice to set him up independently by the gift of a small estate which his energy and ability were to enlarge. Any dowry brought him by his wife was doubtless devoted to this purpose.

The daughter left the house upon marriage and entered her husband's house—or, better, his father's. No other form of emancipation from parental control was known. If she was divorced, she returned discredited and humiliated, to her father's house, and if she married again, had doubtless to descend socially to do so. Divorce, however, may not always have carried this stigma, especially when no moral blame could attach to the woman. So that the state of perpetual tutelage which in the minds of most ancient nations was woman's proper position was likewise her ordinary position in Israel. We ought to remember, however, that this was principally for her protection. A man-child was the desire of every woman as of every man, but the hearts of parents were not closed to their daughters. Jephthah's daughter was an only child and perhaps exceptional; but we may recall the ewe lamb of Nathan's parable, that was to its owner "as a daughter." We may be sure that the affection of fathers was not limited by the fact that only a son would really maintain his name among the people.

Nor did a girl's marriage or her father's death deprive her of natural protectors. Her husband was her master, her *ba'al*, but the house she left continued to watch over her. She had brothers, perhaps, who would drastically resent any real injury done her. The injury contemplated was not so much ill usage as the loss of standing caused by taking new wives into the household. At any rate, a family did not like to marry its women far off, lest they be beyond the protection of their blood.

The ancient Israelites reared all their children. This seems to us so simple and a matter of course that its special mention may cause surprise. But we must remember that it was in direct contradiction with the customs of the entire Mediterranean and particularly with those of the Greeks and Romans whom we know so well. The Romans and Greeks reared only some of their children. The father might and occasionally did reject a child and order it to be exposed. Indeed the fact that the Jews did not was so marked a characteristic of them that all strangers comment upon it —generally with great approbation. Whether the reason for it was the desire to make good by numbers what they lacked in wealth or military power may well be doubted. A large population inevitably invited emigration and until very late, meant the weakening of the people. In fact, it could scarcely be till the complete religious reorganization carried out by Josiah, that a Jew who took up residence among a foreign people would not, almost immediately, cease to feel himself a Jew. The reason for this difference between gentile and Jewish habit is probably to be sought in the religious commands, so frequently repeated in the Bible, which enjoin the utmost fruitfulness, and which promise so large a blessing to the father of many children. Nor ought we to disregard the fact that alone of all religions in their part of the world, that of the Israelites commanded protection of the helpless, even to the extent of exciting the derision of tough-minded gentlemen in that day and this.

Those who insist upon explaining every institution by economics, that is, by ascribing to it an intention of increasing material wealth, may comfort themselves by finding in the refusal of the Jews to expose their children an additional indication of the family structure of society. Whatever disadvantage a large population might entail for a nation, for a family, especially in primitive times, many children, particularly many sons, meant immediate superiority over a neighboring family unit smaller in size. Nor were daughters wholly without their economic uses. They shared largely in important work in the house and their marriage, as we shall see, brought property to the household and only rarely withdrew property. If this was so, the desire of each family to increase would be sanctioned by religion and become a fundamental institution even after the family in its smaller or larger form lost something of its conscious independence; although, we must remember, it never wholly lost it.

Not only did the Jews never expose their children as the Greeks and Romans and Egyptians did, but they did not practise the still more hideous custom of sacrificing them, as did their Canaanite kinsmen and neighbors. This must be stated with emphasis, since it is often asserted, in the face of positive evidence, that such sacrifices were a part of early Jewish custom. It may well be that individual Jews occasionally did this dreadful thing—individual Jews did not scruple at all times to disregard their national and religious laws, even those that prohibited the three abominations, murder, idolatry and incest. But it is fairly certain that they did not think that they were following a national custom or performing a national rite. On the contrary, they did so in deliberate disregard of an emphatic religious precept to refrain.

And this applies not only to the grisly horror of the Moloch sacrifices, but also to the less revolting but equally cruel practice of burying infants alive, as the Phoenicians seem to have done. Of this no trace appears anywhere in the Bible.

The birth of a child was greeted with great rejoicing. If it was a male child the festive character was no doubt enhanced. The day of birth is a proverbial expression for an occasion of great joy. It was thereafter a holy day for the person, celebrated in some ceremonial either of festivity or thanksgiving. It does not seem that gifts were then made as is our custom, although the making of gifts was exceedingly common.

As in the case of other nations there were many customs, some religious and some sanitary, that were observed at a child's birth. The new born child was washed for cleansing, rubbed with salt and then swaddled in linen. The mother, in the case of a boy, could not leave her room for one week; in the case of a girl for two. She was, according to ancient ideas, *taboo*, "unclean," during that period, an idea prevalent over practically the whole world and expressing the thought that at such moments there is something uncanny or abnormal and therefore dangerous about the person affected. At the close of that time, she becomes "clean" again or normal by a duly performed rite of sacrifice and ablution.

On the eighth day a male child was circumcised, an occasion which was apparently wholly religious and was not celebrated with any form of family festivity. Similarly at the redemption of the first-born thirty days thereafter, there was not, so far as we can see, any special rejoicing. It was solely a matter of ritual.

Children might be given out to nurse or be nursed by a female slave, but in most cases mothers nursed their own children. If there was a nurse she became, as among the Greeks, a second mother, bound by almost as close a tie to her nursling as the actual mother was. We remember how Deborah, the nurse of Rebekah, follows her from Padan-aram to Canaan and is buried with filial piety at the "oak of weeping."

The first great festivity in a child's life was its weaning, doubtless as a means of rejoicing in its successful passing through this dangerous crisis in its life. From that time on, apparently, the likelihood of its growing up to full age seemed established. Perhaps it was the inherent perils of this period in the child's life that made mothers postpone the weaning for a long period, sometimes as long as three years. The dangers that might follow from such a course, were not so evident as those that faced the child immediately upon being weaned.

We hear little in the Bible of childish games and toys, just as we hear little of such things in Homer.

Yet children, both boys and girls, played commonly, we are told, in the streets and marketplaces, played doubtless as their elders apparently did, with singing and dancing. Not only were deference and obedience demanded of them but moral responsibility was early laid upon them; yet it is likely that the effort to turn children into miniature adults was as unsuccessful then as it is now. Probably children were on the whole as generally decorous and respectful as they are today in Oriental communities. But the irrepressible irreverence of youth is often mentioned and where they had any adult sanction for scoffing, Hebrew children availed themselves of it fully.

Of schools in biblical times we hear nothing. Children were educated by their parents or by trusted slaves. As has been said, corporal chastisement was not infrequent. Toward the close of biblical times Ben Sira advocated the utmost severity in dealing with children, although he demanded of them unlimited filial devotion and affection. But Ben Sira was a solemn and somewhat opinionated old man who, as he himself tells us, would neither laugh nor play with his children for fear of imperilling his much prized dignity. Not all Jewish fathers can have been of this sort. Tenderness or affection and delight in the mere presence of children are frequently emphasized, and even professional and rigorous moralists had no doubt that spiritual restraints were better than corporeal ones.

The Bible has several references to the noisy games of children in public places. When the prophet promises the restoration of Jerusalem, this is the picture that occurs to his mind, "And the streets of the city shall be full of boys and girls playing in the streets thereof." Also when Job speaks of the prosperity of the wicked he says, "They send forth their little ones like a flock and their children dance." Perhaps they danced to each other's pipings, as they certainly did when they were older, and if so, the dance probably resembled "Here We Go Round The Mulberry Bush" more than anything else.

Unless human beings have changed in essence in thirty centuries, of which there is no evidence, much of their playing was the unregulated romping and hallooing that have always been the outlet of youthful exuberance. Doubtless they became sedate and restrained at an earlier age than our children do, but that is merely another way of saying that Mediterraneans have an earlier maturity than we have. Of one thing we may be sure. We ought not to fill our imaginations with the conventional picture of biblical children—sad, solemn and retired—except when evoked for purposes of admonition.

The members of the family group have not been completely enumerated. Besides the father and mother and children, there are two additional classes which almost every ancient society knew. One consisted of slaves, the other of resident aliens, "the strangers within the gates."

Slavery in the ancient Mediterranean world was so universal that the great Aristotle could not imagine human society without it. In theory, of course, a slave was a chattel, a thing, no less and no more so than an ox or a sheep; but it was reserved for nineteenth century slaveholders in the southern states of America to carry that theory into a cruelly logical practice. The great difference between ancient and modern slavery was this: the ancient slave was obviously of the same stock as his master, as far as that could be determined by physical criteria. The thought could scarcely arise therefore that the slave was a creature necessarily and permanently inferior.

Again, the ancient slave was a member of his master's family. That was not altogether true in most parts of Greece and in later Rome. In early Rome, however, and at almost all times among the Jews, the slave's participation in the family group was as full as that of his master's children. Slaves, as has been said, frequently became their masters' wives, their daughters-in-law and their sons-in-law.

In Rome it was not until the second century C. E. that the killing of a slave was made homicide. In Israel, there never was a time when law or practice ignored the human character of this form of property. We cannot suppose that cruel and violent men were lacking among the Jews. Yet complaints that slaves were ill-treated are surprisingly rare. Nor did slavery create a taint that only several generations of subsequent freedom could eradicate. We know that slaves were emancipated, but there is no technical word for emancipated slave, such as we have in Greek and Latin. Apparently they formed no special class, but disappeared in the mass of free citizens.

The exact legal position of slaves, whether Hebrew or gentile, is somewhat difficult to make out. It is a much controverted question. In the Sabbatical year, that is every seventh year, and in the Jubilee, that is every fiftieth year, Hebrew slaves were required by law to be set free unless they voluntarily chose to remain slaves. Unfortunately, this was not always done. Once when in a fit of repentance King Zedekiah ordered the law to be observed, the freed slaves were again reduced to bondage when the repentance was over. Was the law on this matter merely a moral precept which the pious would observe and the indifferent disregard? It is more likely that it was a formally complete law, but that negligentmagistrates failed to enforce it, as they failed to enforce other laws.

Between slavery proper and a qualified form of bondage as a security for debt, the Bible does not distinguish in words, and men scarcely distinguished in practice. When amidst the "Sundry Proverbs" we read that the "borrower is the servant of the lender," that is to be taken in a painfully literal sense. To borrow money was no light thing in the ancient world. A man who could not pay, could not simply declare himself a bankrupt and suffer merely an impairment of credit. If he failed to meet his obligation, there was the man himself and—it is regrettably but undeniably true—there were those who belonged to him, and the heavy hand of the creditor fell upon all of them.

One of the most striking illustrations is the incident related in II Kings, Chapter 4. "Now there cried a certain woman of the wives of the sons of the prophets unto Elisha, saying, 'Thy servant my husband is dead and thou knowest that thy servant did fear the Lord and the creditor is come to take unto him my two sons to be bondmen'." The story goes on to tell how Elisha miraculously increased the little store of oil till it filled many vessels and then told her, "Go sell the oil and pay thy debt." We notice that the creditor made no attempt to seize any of her property but was about to take her sons at once.

What would have happened to them? In some parts of the world there was the pleasant theory that these unhappy people could work off their debt, that in some ways their services would be assessed and deducted from the debt and the accrued interest. Somehow that rarely happened and debt-slavery meant for all practical purposes a permanent bondage.

But in Israel there was apparently not even that theory. It would seem that upon failure to pay, the debtor could be incontinently seized. If then out of

the sale of his property or out of the contributions of
his kin, he could pay the debt, he might claim to be
released. Otherwise he remained in slavery until such
redemption took place. The difference, therefore, between a real slave and a debtor slave was merely in
this right of redemption.

But even such a right of redemption was nugatory
if the creditor sold his human security, and doubly
futile, if he sold him into foreign slavery. To be sure
he was required by law not to do this, but he was
required by law not to sell him at all, but to keep him
as a day-laborer only. Yet of the three and four transgressions of Israel, against which Amos thundered,
two are that "they have sold the righteous for silver
and the needy for a pair of shoes." And in the admira-
ble diary of Nehemiah we hear how the poor were sold
in defiance of the law.

Those who obeyed the law in this respect no doubt
often exacted their legal rights even against the righteous and the needy, but the status of the unfortunate
debtor would with such creditors more nearly resemble
that of dependents, of clients, than of slaves.

A real group of clients was to be met in those so
often called the "strangers," especially "the stranger
that is within thy gates." Except for the constant
recrudescence of anti-foreign agitations in the United
States, we might almost forget that there was a time
when between a foreigner and a countryman there was
a great gulf. In the Germanic North, the foreigner was

"outside the peace," a "wolf." He might be killed with impunity. In a measure that was everywhere true, and voyages to a foreign land had many more dangers than the ordinary perils of travel. But from time immemorial, in the eastern Mediterranean, nations that boasted of their civilization boasted particularly of this indication of it: that a suppliant or inoffensive stranger was under a divine protection and that to injure him was an impiety of the most serious kind.

Of course between strangers there were differences. There was the stranger who retained his nationality and who came only by chance and for a brief period into the land, the *nokri*. Even he might be allowed some part in the divine worship, and of some such strangers the Bible gives instances of particular loyalty and devotion to the country or person who harbored them. Ittai, the man of Gath, swears to David "as the Lord liveth" as zealously as David himself might have sworn the great oath, and of that abhorrence of strangers with which the Jews were absurdly credited in ancient times and present, there is no real trace in the Bible.

As for the other stranger, the sojourner, the stranger within the gates, the foreigner who came into the land to stay there, it may be safely said that nowhere in the world of his time was he so protected or so secure. He was emphatically within and not without the peace of the land. "Ye shall have one manner of law as well for the stranger as for one of your own country," says one of the many codes in our Bible; and the spirit is true of all of them. He needed no individual protector, though he most frequently had one. He might wax rich and powerful. He might even acquire an Israelitish debtor as bond-servant. And above all, he was to suffer no wrong. "Thou shalt neither vex a stranger nor oppress him." This injunction occurs often, and frequently there is coupled with it the sentence, "For ye were strangers in the land of Egypt." The reason is the afterthought. From the first, it is evident the tribesmen of the Covenant carried into the land they dominated the ancient custom of their desert, that he who came near with words of peace could claim as of right the shelter and protection of the tent. "Love ye the stranger," Deuteronomy demands, "for the Lord your God, the God of gods and Lord of lords—He loveth the stranger."

He has a real if limited share in the divine communion. The Sabbath is for him as well as for the Jew. He appears before Jehovah as his hosts do. He shares in the blessings for obedience and the punishment for disobedience. He might intermarry with Jews. It is contemplated that a priest's daughter might have such a stranger as her husband. And there can be scarcely any doubt that if not he himself, his son almost certainly became merged completely into the nation that had received him.

In most cases, the stranger within the gates came even more closely than by mere physical presence into the community. He became an actual member of the household of some *ba'al ha-bayit*. He was some one's stranger. "Thy stranger," says the Decalogue, is to observe the Sabbath. If he was outside the household, he was likely to be, not indeed without protection, but in the same class as the poor, the fatherless and the widow, wards of the nation as a whole, for whom the corners of the fields are to be left and the surplus of the vines. If, however, he is some man's stranger or client, he has an assured place in the community. He relies not merely on the moral sense of the people for his protection, but on the often substantial power of the house into which he has entered.

The family was a unit in the completest way conceivable, and its unity was centered in the personality of its head. Just as the house was his, so its wrongs were his. The *ba'al* suffered, not vicariously but directly, when that house was injured. Its obligations were his obligations. It was Job who was smitten when his children were killed, just as Job's prayers made good those his sons might have omitted. We do not quite get a full conception of the matter by supposing him simply the intercessor for his sons or grieving for them as a man might grieve for the loss of some one he loved.

This solidarity of the family was carried to an extreme that gives us a certain shock. Achan, who touched the accursed thing, was stoned with his sons and daughters, his oxen and sheep. When Naboth was put to death, wickedly enough but in the forms of law, he suffered with his sons. It was a cruel old superstition working here, that guilt contaminated, and the master and his household were one.

But evidently this age-old superstition shocked the Jews too, at a time when it was still a matter of course to most of the world. 'Joash, King of Judah, was assassinated by his servants and his son Amaziah avenged him, as was to be expected. But, it is stated, "the children of the murderers he slew not: according to that which is written in the book of the law of Moses, wherein the Lord commanded, saying, 'The fathers shall not be put to death for the children nor the children for the fathers, but each man shall be put to death for his own sin'." The book in question is Deuteronomy (24, 16), and it is frequently asserted that Deuteronomy is to be dated about 625 B. C. E. This incident, however, took place two hundred years earlier. Whether Deuteronomy is or is not of the date mentioned, the Amaziah incident can scarcely be an invention, and if a king could refuse to avenge his father by the blood of the innocent, it goes far to prove that the responsibility of the family as a whole for transgressions of any member had been seriously lessened in very ancient times. How ancient those times were we may understand when we remember that we have Athenian laws of 400 B. C. E., two hundred years after the latest date given to Deuteronomy, which prescribe punishment for a criminal and his whole family and that fifty years later Plato can take for granted that the wife and children of a traitor will suffer the horrible death penalty for treason together with the guilty man.

Family unity and solidarity were ideas that seemed grounded in the foundations of the world. They died hard, or rather they have not died out yet, even in ultra-modern communities. But the first breach that was made in the solid wall was made by those fierce tribesmen who had made a covenant in the desert with a compassionate and merciful God.

CHAPTER IV

MARRIAGE

THE family, as we have seen, was the unit of ancient society, not the individual. And if we have appeared to lay undue stress on the individuals that composed it—the father, the mother, the children, the slaves, the strangers—we have after all spoken of these individuals only in what we may call their social aspect.

At the present time we still recognize the family as the cardinal institution of modern society, although its composition is somewhat different. Our family is based on marriage; a valid marriage is its foundation and few if any of the family relations ordinarily arise in any other way. Of the Israelites this was not so at all. The family was the *ba'al* and his *bayit*, the master and his household. Obviously some of the members were his wives, but there might be wedded couples within his house who did not form families at all. So far was marriage from being the foundation of the family that it seemed rather an incident in one's life like the redemption of the first born or weaning or any other physical or social stage of development.

Still it was a highly important incident, however much it retained the character of something that happened to a man or woman rather than anything they did. Under normal circumstances, one master said to another, "Give thy daughter to my son to wife." And if the one addressed consented, the young people were betrothed by this contract between their parents. The betrothed girl, *arusah*, was in legal contemplation already a wife. Infidelity on her part was adultery. In fact all the legal consequences of marriage flowed from this contract in which those whom we should regard as most concerned had never a word to say.

The "marriage" itself was a festive occasion, a feast that marked the beginning of cohabitation. It had no special religious ceremony but it quickly gathered about itself a host of gay customs, some of them immemorial in the land. It added nothing whatever to the rights and duties of the parties. But obviously it was one of the great days in the lives of both the man and the woman, a "day of gladness of heart."

These marriage customs most frequently took the form of a ceremonious bringing home of the bride. Both bride and bridegroom were decked as they never were before and perhaps would not be again, in regal splendor, and were joyously acclaimed as king and queen. The most widely accepted interpretation of the Song of Songs is that it is a series of songs chanted on just such an occasion by the bridegroom and his attendants, to which the bride and her maidens replied in kind. The bridegroom went forth with his companions—thirty accompanied Samson—and was met by the veiled and splendidly attired bride surrounded by her friends. Then, with songs that filled the streets, in which doubtless all the unoccupied joined whether invited guests or not, the bride was escorted to her new home. There a wedding feast was held that sometimes lasted a week and more. These feasts with their local and homely associations loomed large in the lives of a toilsome people. When the prophet threatens woe to his people, the voice he will make cease is the voice of "gladness and mirth," the "voice of the bridegroom and of the bride."

The real marriage contract, the betrothal, was, it has been said, made for the bridegroom and the bride by their fathers. Yet there were instances in which the contracting party spoke in his own name. A man might, if he were himself a *ba'al ha-bayit*, the head of a household, take wives for himself. And of course this must have happened often enough. In such a case there was still a real contract of betrothal. But there was no real contract when the father selected a female slave as his son's wife or a male slave as his daughter's husband. Obviously that worked an emancipation of the slave and the marriage then differed in no respect from the ordinary type.

Even before a man was really the head of a household he might be sufficiently independent to take or receive a wife for himself. If he were in the king's service, whether as warrior or official, that was enough to free him from his father's control. Certainly it does not appear that the consent of Jesse was asked when Saul gave Michal to David, or that the promise of Caleb to Othniel needed confirmation by the latter's father. The point is that the relation between a young soldier and his captain was almost that of father and son. Saul and David address each other as "My father" and "My son," and that apparently for a more intimate reason than because of the general protection of a king over his subjects.

However, it is not as father but as head of the house that a man gives wives to his sons and gives his daughters to other men. A woman might do so if she were a widow and her authority would extend both to her actual children and to those who bore that relation to her. Hagar selects a wife for Ishmael and if Naomi does not exactly give Ruth to Boaz, that is because of the complicated rules as to the next of kin, who had a right to marry Ruth if he chose. It is evident that the marriage price, of which we must speak hereafter, would have gone to Naomi.

All this dwelling on legal requirements makes us prone to forget the normal affections that exist in a family. A father was not legally required to seek his son's or daughter's approval for the spouse he selected, but we may be sure he often did. Rebekah was asked, "Wilt thou go with this man?" before she was sent to her husband. It is true that the stories of the ancient princesses of the people are no safe guides, but this is a human touch which we shall forego with reluctance.

In the same story, although Bethuel, Rebekah's father, was living, her brother and mother have a voice in her bestowal. And yet this voice was apparently only advisory. The matter had already really been settled. Rebekah herself later on was not so fortunate in one of her sons, who took to wife two of the daughters of Heth, "which were a grief of mind unto Isaac and Rebekah." Esau apparently was competent to contract an independent marriage, but as the story is told, it is doubtless intended to convey the impression that his conduct was a brutal disregard of propriety.

A great deal has been written about the survival in Israel of an earlier form of family. This form has no technical name, but the social structure of which it was a part is called the matriarchate. It implies that the women were at one time quite independent; indeed, that they formed the only stable elements in the family group, that relationship was traced through them and property derived from them. Many writers of the last generation believed that the matriarchate was a necessary stage in the evolution of society everywhere and that numerous traces or vestiges of that stage are to be met with in the customs of almost every people. There seems no reason to believe that this is so, but it is undoubtedly true that among many existing and vanished nations women played an altogether different rôle in family life from that just described or from that familiar to us. And that rôle was somewhat like the position of women in the imaginary matriarchate. They were important as a class, even where individuals were as restricted and limited in activity as the women of the Bible.

Did the ancient Semites, the ancestors of the invading Hebrews, or the ancient Canaanites, whom they subdued and absorbed, have a tradition of such an earlier family? If they did it would be indicated by a type of marriage in which the woman retained actual control of her property and above all remained mistress of her house, into which she received her husband as a visitor. Now it cannot be denied that some of the biblical stories seem to imply such a custom. Sarah, for instance, has her own tent and her slaves. She disposes of one of these slaves, cruelly enough to our way of thinking, against the remonstrance of Abraham. But we must bear in mind a caution already alluded to. Sarah in legend and heroic song was a very exceptional person, the "princess," and those who told and heard these stories thought of their ancestress in terms quite different from those they would apply to flesh and blood human beings.

A marriage of the kind dear to anthropologists occurs in another story. Samson marries a Philistine woman but does not take her to his home. Instead he visits her in her father's house on relatively rare occasions. Our record calls this a marriage and the Timnathite woman is referred to as Samson's wife and not his concubine. Samson, it is true, is the most mythical of all the Jewish heroes, but if this marriage had been wholly strange, some reference would have been made to its peculiar character. Evidently it was not unfamiliar. Perhaps it was recognized only when an alien woman was concerned and marriages with aliens were dealt with even more summarily than others. If it really existed as a type of union, it had no importance.

For poetry and romance, a marriage is the leaping together of two kindred souls that recognize each other almost immediately. In the regulated social structure of almost any nation, it is a contract, and a contract unfortunately calls to mind unpleasant commercial images. One of the least unpleasant of these is the institution called the dowry. That word is applied in English speaking countries to a gift made to the husband by the bride's father or family. It has no legal or social importance and has a certain taint about it, in that it implies mercenary motives in the bridegroom and lack of personal attraction in the bride. In Continental Europe the dowry is free from any such taint. It is the contribution the bride's family makes to the expenses of the new household. The husband has merely the administration of the dowry and at the dissolution of the marriage by death or divorce, it goes back to its source.

Now when a real dowry is met with in the Bible it is of this sort. Perhaps it was not really a Jewish practice, but one belonging to the surrounding society, especially the Egyptians and Babylonians. Yet it is spoken of as though it would be recognized as a definite and familiar institution. By the time of Ben Sira, it was fairly common, and it had produced the same result as in a later time at Rome. The well-dowered wife was prone to be domineering, since the property she brought could be used by the husband only as a sort of trust and watchful eyes would demand an accounting. "Desire not a woman for her possessions," he warns us, "since it is slavery and a reproach if a woman maintain her husband."

Yet, also as at Rome, it must have served the beneficent purpose of checking the fatally easy divorce which gave husbands such power over their wives. There is little indication in the Bible that this evil was a specially serious one, but there must have been occasional instances of heartless divorces, and in later times the dowry institution must have helped to restrict them.

However, the word "dowry" that appears in our English Bible is the translation of two very different words. The one, *zebed*, is the dowry proper which has just been discussed. The other, much more frequently used word, is *mohar*, which does not mean dowry at all, but something quite different, "the marriage price." However much we should like to have it otherwise, the ancient marriage throughout that part of the world was a purchase and was frankly so considered. Homer calls girls "cattle-bringing," which means that suitors paid for them in what was then equivalent to money, so that fair daughters were a source of profit to the Homeric chieftain. It was clearly so in Israel and the words "sell" and "buy" continued to be used of giving and taking in marriage long after the later dowry institution had become fairly universal.

The *mohar* was paid by the groom or by his father to the father of the girl. In the seventh century B.C.E. an average *mohar* seems to have been fifty shekels of silver, something like twenty dollars; but, of course, it had many times the present purchasing power of that sum.

Now, to class women as commodities that can be sold and delivered is degrading enough in all conscience, and yet from what has been seen, the position of women was far from being degraded in Israel. Institutions, after all, depend for their significance not on their form but upon the people who administer them. If an ancient Hebrew followed an immemorial and almost universal custom in paying "shekels of silver current money with the merchants" for his wife, he intended to make of her not the minister of his conveniences but a participant in the divine communion he boasted of enjoying. She like him is to appear before the Lord, to hear His Law and to be trained in fear of Him.

Indeed it is easily possible that the marriage price or *mohar* was quite generally treated as a means of compensating for a legal disability which was regarded as a serious injustice. Daughters received nothing

from their father's estate by way of inheritance. The
Jews found this rule and did not make it and it was
too firmly fixed in the habits of society to be changed.
But that it disturbed them may be gathered from the
story of the daughters of Zelophehad in Numbers. And
this *mohar* or marriage price had, at least by the eighth
century, come to be regarded as a trust held by the
father for the married daughter, to be restored to her
on his death.   Apparently that is what Leah and
Rachel mean when they ask, "Is there yet portion or
inheritance for us in our father's house?—He hath
sold us and hath quite devoured our money." The
deceitful Laban might well do this without fear of
legal consequences, but the moral disrepute that would
follow would doubtless have checked an ordinary man.

Instead of money a wife might be earned by services.
Jacob in the well-known story served seven years for
Leah and seven for Rachel. Similarly the first Judge,
Othniel, earned his bride by a feat of arms, and David
"bought" Saul's daughter by slaughtering Philistines.
And in the case of Jacob and Othniel they receive
brides and valuable possessions for the same services.
We may be tempted to suppose that in this story we
have the origin of the later dowry, the marriage portion proper, since we can readily believe that the
earning of a bride by services was not uncommon.

There is also another type of wife, the concubine.
The word for it in the Bible, *pilegesh*, is curiously
un-Hebrew in appearance and may be borrowed with

the institution it represents from foreign nations, but certainly the concubine cannot be a strange figure in a society that permitted polygamy. Concubines existed in ancient Rome in spite of its theoretical monogamy, and everywhere the difference between a wife and a concubine was less the ceremony which created the relation than the rank of the person who entered into it. Certain women, it seems, could not be wives, but merely concubines, of men of higher social position.

That is intelligible enough for kings and princes, but the Levite in the tragic and bloody story told in the later chapters of Judges also had a concubine and he was certainly of no high social rank. When we remember that the marriage of slave-women to free-men is contemplated as a possibility and that such a marriage makes the woman a wife, not a concubine, the distinction is hard to make out, unless we are dealing with the ideas of different ages. Otherwise we might guess that concubinage was the only relation possible between a man and a woman who was completely outside of some family bond—a stranger without a patron, let us say, or a woman whose kinsmen were all dead. Ruth, for example, had Naomi died before she encountered Boaz, could scarcely have become Boaz's full wife.

Probably the marriage that was most clearly a marriage of equals was that between cousins. Instances of it abound. It is so definitely the ideal marriage in all that part of the world that later Arabs addressed their wives by the courtesy title of "daughter of my uncle." Then, too, marriages between half-brothers and sisters on the father's side were legal as late as the exile, as they were legal in Athens at a much later period. Such kinship was not so visibly close as it seems to us, for in a polygamous household children of different mothers dwelt apart from each other. We may give this tendency to marry within the group the fine anthropological name of endogamy, but it was probably not a conscious system, merely the result of ordinary prudence. Brothers would seek to unite their children in order to keep family property together, or because they had greater confidence in brides or bridegrooms whose antecedents they knew. Whatever we call this system, we must remember that giving it a name does not of itself explain it.

CHAPTER V

EDUCATION

THE prophetic picture of a prosperous and happy city stresses the fact that the city shall be full of boys and girls playing in the streets thereof. Modern children might look longingly back toward a past in which it was assumed that they would have no other business than that of irresponsible playing, when they had not yet become the subjects of scientific study nor of exact regulation. And unless our memories play us tricks, that ancient day will seem particularly pleasant if our children are told that there were then no schools.

In fact the very word "school" does not occur in either the Bible or the Apocrypha in any sense at all resembling our modern meaning. Jewish tradition asserted that the first school in Palestine was founded by Simeon b. Shetah about 75 B. C. E. Elsewhere it is said that Joshua b. Gamala in 60 C. E. provided a great many schools for the whole country. The tradition seems in both cases to be based on authentic records and is quite consistent with the facts that we know. Both of these dates are, of course, long after the biblical period, and confirm the inference of the non-existence of schools which we drew from the silence of our records.

But if there were no schools, there was a great deal of teaching, if we assume that biblical precepts were followed. "These words," says Deuteronomy, "thou shalt teach diligently unto thy children." And under "these words" are evidently understood "the commandments, the statutes and the judgements" which fill the many chapters of that book. In fact the duty to teach is one of the most important and repeated of the "commandments" which, in the talmudic phrase, God multiplied upon Israel for His Name's sake and for Israel's glory.

This teaching, of course, was wholly ethical. Right conduct was taught, and, in later times, doubtless those incidents in Jewish history which illustrated and enforced the divine precepts. But the teaching was not done in schools, but at home by the father and the mother, the duty evidently devolving upon both of them in equal measure.

What comes into our minds at once is whether all parents acquitted themselves well of the duty imposed upon them. We have the uneasy consciousness that a not dissimilar duty is by common opinion placed upon modern parents and that it is not particularly well done. And even such moral instruction as actually takes place at the present time consists rather in the direction of conduct, in the formation of certain habits, than in set instruction. Direction like this occurred in biblical times as well and is called "teaching" in the Bible as it is now. But the word used for it is the

Hebrew word *horah*, not the more common word *limmad*. When Deuteronomy speaks of "teaching" in the passage quoted, the writer means a real instruction, an imparting of the actual substance of the "statutes, commandments and judgements," so that they might in turn be handed down to the next generation.

We should certainly not like to rely on individual parents for instruction of this sort at the present time, and we may properly wonder whether those who relied on them in the seventh century B. C. E. were better advised. If we turn again to that exemplary and somewhat put upon person, the Woman of Valour of Proverbs, this function of the mother is, I think, indicated in the verse, "She openeth her mouth with wisdom and in her tongue is the law of kindness." Obviously, the *eshet hayil* would do so; but was every woman that? The author of this Song and Ben Sira both indicate that they thought her a rarity.

And for the fathers themselves, may we suppose that a very large number spent some part of each day in specific instruction of their children? Certainly a great many more did so than do so now, but if the fulminations of prophets are to be believed, there were many who were delinquent in most of the "commandments," and who cannot be credited with having observed this one. We shall see that certain classes found it necessary to make such work their special business and that their pupils were not children.

Some children, then, were taught, if not all, and they were taught the Torah, the sum of the laws and statutes. Were they taught anything else? Was there anything that corresponded to the three R's of our education? It does not seem that there was. At any rate, there was surely no set group of subjects which we may suppose every child or most children had to pass through as an almost inevitable incident of their childhood. Doubtless a man who could read taught his children to do so—feeling probably as he would toward any other form of skill or craftsmanship that he possessed. But how many men were literate? There were surely few ready writers among the warriors who followed Joshua across the Jordán, who sacked Jericho and Ai and smote the five Kings at Gibeon. And throughout the periods of greater prosperity, knowledge of this mistress art must have been an exception. It is taken for granted that both family and public instruction shall be oral. The learned man reads and the congregation hears and perpends.

Yet Isaiah in 680 B. C. E. assumes that reading and writing are fairly common. It is of course true that he is speaking of the city, of Jerusalem. We do not know just how far "common script" was really common elsewhere. Isaiah in the same passages distinguishes between the learned who can read and the unlearned who cannot. Outside of Jerusalem it is not to be supposed that shepherd and peasant knew or wanted letters.

Just what the method of instruction was we can only guess. The Bible tells us nothing about it, but the most reasonable guess is that it was largely oral. Frequently young men are admonished to "give heed and listen," "to give ear," and the like. This points to oral instruction. Evidently repetition and drill were the chief devices used just as they have been the fundaments of educational technique ever since. We know a great deal more about Greek teaching from about 500 B. C. E. on, and we know that among the Greeks the pupil stood before his master and repeated after him the passages his teacher recited. Evidently that was also the manner of Hebrew teaching.

What was taught took the form of proverbs, like those in the book of that name, or in Ben Sira. These proverbs are in verse, we may remember; we can hardly believe that such difficult and dry material could have been kept in young minds at all unless it had been in verse. "Write ye this song for you and teach it," says Deuteronomy—this song being the same commandments that are to be imparted "diligently." Ancient "songs" more obviously poetical in substance were also included in this instruction, like that splendid Song of the Bow which was to be taught to the children of Judah. But prayers and actual laws were cast in the same form and learned by children just as Roman children learned the Twelve Tables or Mohammedan children learn the Koran and Jewish children in the *heder* learn the Pentateuch at this very day.

Much depended—indeed far too much—on sheer strength of memory. The Greeks too thought of memory as a high mental quality and not a low one, and termed it the Mother of the Muses. At a little later time it was said of R. Eliezer b. Hyrkanos that he retained all that had been taught him, and this test of a good pupil is undoubtedly ancient. Yet we may properly say that education was severely practical. To do the will of God one must know it, but the performance was the only important thing. Obviously erudition in such matters could not have been regarded as an end in itself in the earlier times. Even when men had become more sophisticated and schools abounded, the purpose of teaching was not lost sight of. "Not learning but doing is the chief thing," said R. Simeon b. Gamaliel, voicing a warning that must have been necessary when the statutes and commandments had become very numerous. The disillusioned author of Ecclesiastes—one of the latest books of our Bible—found that increase of knowledge was increase of sorrow, but this form of elegant pessimism is almost inevitable in cultured communities, and even Koheleth would not have foregone the wisdom he found so vexatious of spirit.

Quite apart from this form of teaching which was in theory the right of every child, was a specialized teaching which certain particular children received.

From the beginning of history, we meet men of a special craft. These were not only the masters of the fine arts—of which the most notable example was music—but of every form of technical skill. Later they included men called Scribes or Writers and very soon those that were called the "Prophets" or the "Wise."

Now any man who possessed a kind of skill that was hard to acquire called it a "mystery" and treated it as such. He transmitted it to his son or if he took a stranger in, that stranger became in effect a son and often formally adopted. Two crafts were by tradition especially ancient; they were "those that handle the harp and organ," the sons of Jubal, and the "artificers in brass and iron," the sons of Tubal-Cain. Of the character and position of these and other crafts we must speak in another place. We are concerned with them now only as illustrations of a special kind of education.

How was technical skill taught? The crafts were of course hereditary, but even the son of a harper will not play at birth or play without instruction. We must assume that the instruction was desperately vocational. Nothing, we may be sure, was farther from the master's mind than a theoretical or systematized teaching. If he was a smith, he welded the iron while his apprentice blew the bellows and the latter was supposed to learn his craft by dint of watching an oft repeated process. It is not really a bad way of learning such things and many men find it the simplest method even at the present time. The speed of acquisition, and the degree of success in practice, depended then, as it does now, on individual aptitudes.

These crafts, it has been said, were very ancient. The "harp or organ" was only one of many musical instruments known in Palestine. We hear of pipes, tabrets, psalteries, cymbals and trumpets. None of them could be played without skill and all therefore implied instruction. Very soon those who played them formed loose corporations; perhaps skill in such things was always the mark of certain clans or family groups. The sons of Asaph were obviously a clan or guild of musicians connected with the temple service. So were the sons of Korah, of Heman, of Ethan. In the Chronicler's account of the discomfiture of Athaliah, he makes explicit mention of a group of teachers of music who were part of the regular temple organization. That may have been true only of post-exilic days. It is not at all unlikely that at that time the young people of the temple servitors were trained together in what would very closely resemble schools, even if they were highly specialized ones.

Of the other crafts, we may say that we can almost see the process of their formation within biblical times. Weaving, tanning, building, spinning, all the things that are done in our day by skilled workmen expert in these arts were originally done in the family circle by women or men belonging to it. But the process of specialization had begun, and to the extent that it had begun, it implied that the special skill which made the craftsman had to be imparted to the apprentice. If the bakers and fullers were as well organized as the more ancient craftsmen, "schools" of these apprentices may be assumed to have existed. But of course, in both cases a "school" was merely a large group of apprentices sent to some one preëminently skilful craftsman. With a little imagination we can see such a group of master and apprentices growing into an excellent counterpart of a modern "industrial" or "technical" school, which is apparently the latest creation of the latest system of education.

Now while that may possibly have happened for the technical arts in Israel in the early days of the settlement, we are not reduced to imagination and probability when we deal with an art which we should not call technical at all, the art of wisdom. Men who were wise, either because like the ancient seers and prophets they spoke with direct inspiration, or because like the later *hakam*, or "wise man," they gave to many the lore acquired by long and painful study of books and deep meditation on God and man—such men seem always to have been present among the Jews in considerable numbers. And always they walked attended by a crowd of disciples whom they called their "sons"—as spiritually they were. These "sons of the prophets" were settled in fixed places, at Gilgal, at Jericho, at Bethel, where, sitting on the ground at the feet of their master, they learned from his eloquent lips many things which they cannot have quite understood but which had the desired effect of stimulating their already highly aroused religious exaltation.

The "sons of the prophets" were grown men, but they were often young men, and they doubtless felt that in a real sense they were completing their education, since, as we have seen, the only formal and conscious teaching they had received as children had been moral and religious.

When the days of prophets and inspired seers had passed, an exactly similar function was fulfilled by the "wise," who taught the law of Moses to eager students .in their homes. But in post-exilic days, when synagogues—or religious corporations—existed everywhere, the function of these wise men was a double one. First, as members and doubtless officers of these synagogues, they taught the people—formally, on the Sabbath, by the method which has maintained itself to the present day—the reading of the Pentateuch and its exposition in the form of a translation and an elucidating sermon. Secondly, they taught in their own houses a select number of men who desired some day to be wise men like their masters.

The public teaching of the people in the synagogue in the years after the Return was a function which the wise either took or usurped from an older group. There were priests before there were wise men and it is very definitely stated that the priests were to teach as well as to sacrifice. In the Book of Chronicles, which we have many reasons for thinking quite late, 350 B. C. E. perhaps, there are several references to this function of the priests. A "teaching priest," the prophet tells King Asa, is wanting in Judah. On another occasion, the Chronicler refers to the "Levites who taught the people." This same allusion to the Levites as teachers occurs in the narrative portion of the Book of Nehemiah which was originally a part of Chronicles. But in Deuteronomy, which is much older, the Levites are also the instructors of the people, although their subject matter is in this passage confined to certain ritual observances. I suppose there was little difference in men's minds between the complicated ritual for a special purpose such as that of which Deuteronomy speaks, and "the good knowledge of the Lord" which, the Chronicler tells us, was also taught by the Levites. All these things constituted the "ancestral wisdom," expounded to the people in the synagogues.

How expounded? In this adult education there was no question of merely observing and imitating. Nor again could it have been enough to be carried by a master's torrential eloquence into a renewed religious enthusiasm, as we may imagine was the case with the "sons of the prophets." When Ezra and the Levites and the wise men of Proverbs taught in public synagogues, the methods they employed were those which are still in vogue. "They taught in Judah and had the book of the law of the Lord with them, and went about throughout all the cities of Judah and taught the people." Just what they did is told us in another passage. "And they read in the book, in the law of God, distinctly; and they gave the sense, and caused them to understand the reading." What was done seems clear enough. A portion of the law was first read in Hebrew, then translated into Aramaic, the language of the people, and finally expounded in a sermon. Evidently the sermon was a *derashah*, like the sermons collected within the next few centuries into the existing Midrashim.

If teaching the people had ever been the exclusive privilege of the priests and Levites, it did not long remain so. The class of the scribes, the instructed men, of whom Ezra was an outstanding representative, recruited their numbers from priests and non-priests. At the close of the biblical period the latter seem to have outnumbered the former. A few centuries later the scribes and the priests are almost in organized opposition to each other. The priestly caste, when it became powerful, suffered the fate of all ruling castes. It became corrupt and mercenary. Long before the Exile the exploitation of the priestly office for personal enrichment had been denounced by Micah. "The heads thereof judge for reward and the priests thereof teach for hire and the prophets thereof divine for money." The teaching of children ultimately became a recognized calling, though we cannot suppose it was a very lucrative one. The teaching of adults did not become such a calling until long after biblical times. It had once been an important part of a holy office, and turning it into a source of profit never ceased to be discreditable.

CHAPTER VI

CITY AND COUNTRY

WHO built the first city? Cain, the first murderer, says the Book of Genesis (4, 17). [It may be remarked that to modern critics, this is one of the oldest parts of the Bible.] It is possible that there was an old tradition according to which Cain, despite his wickedness, was none the less the ancestor of mankind and his children the founders of civilization. However, in this passage we seem to see a still older tradition which thought of the city as an invention of evil men, the abode of insolence and violence, while in the fields and tents dwelt simplicity and righteousness. Those uncompromising zealots for the Lord, the sons of Rechab, lived all their lives in tents, builded no houses, planted no vineyards, and maintained uncorrupted the immemorial custom of the Covenanters with whom they had joined themselves.

But when we first hear of the Rechabites, in the ninth century B. C. E., their manner of life was already a curious survival. All the rest of Israel sowed seed, planted vineyards, built houses and dwelt in them, and the ancient mistrust and fear of cities had practically disappeared. Men were never allowed to forget that the proper and most acceptable condition of the people of God was that of wandering shepherds. But, after all, these shepherds had been sent by the Lord to possess the land and the land was one of fenced cities, great and powerful, of fertile valleys as well as rich pastures. In one of the oldest, the largest, the strongest of these fenced cities was the Holy House itself, soon the only place where God might be properly worshipped. So they compromised with their memories by revering the Rechabites for their persistent loyalty to the ancient manner but imitating them only on the great Feast of the Autumn Ingathering, on Sukkot.

Most of the cities of Palestine were older than the Invasion, whether that took place in a single flood, or came in successive waves. But in a few generations the Israelites had made themselves thoroughly comfortable in the cities of the Jebusites and Ammonites, even before we can assume that the process of assimilating these older inhabitants had gone very far. Perhaps it was in these cities more than elsewhere that the process of assimilation worked in the opposite direction, and made Canaanites out of the Covenanters. Yet this contrary movement must have gone on in the country as well as in the city, since the routine of agriculture was as foreign to the original tribesmen as city life itself. It is likely that in the cities they were more subject to those general influences that pervaded the whole region, influences that emanated from the ancient centers of civilization in Mesopotamia and on the Nile, from Asia Minor and finally and overwhelmingly from the Greek coasts and islands.

Hundreds of cities are referred to in the Bible and many of them are named, besides towns and villages in great numbers. But old records are likely to be somewhat unreliable in such enumerations. Can we really suppose that in the days of Moses there were in Bashan alone sixty "cities" besides towns and villages? There were certainly nothing like so many in the season of Bashan's later prosperity. And the same must be said of those many cities cited in the Book of Joshua.

Yet after all our skepticism is aroused only because a city seems to us a very considerable place. It suggests Paris, New York, London, and we apply the term with reluctance to places of which the population does not run into tens of thousands. An ancient city, however, was not determined by size. It was distinguished from a town or village in a very simple way: it had a wall. We may therefore credit the smallest tribe in Israel with its tale of cities as set forth in the Book of Joshua, if we remember that many of these cities may have been simply clusters of small houses protected by a wall of some sort.

But in every instance that wall was a real wall, built of stone, with gates and towers. It was never a mere stockade or an earthen entrenchment. And if some of the cities were tiny even by ancient standards, some were great cities by all standards—a greatness evidenced by existing ruins if by nothing else. The Davidic kings built the ancient Uru-salim into a mag-

nificent city and the house of Omri placed a splendid
capital on the hill that had belonged to Shemer. And
while Jerusalem and Samaria were the outstanding
cities, many others existed older than either, cities like
Dan, Bethel, Shechem, Rabbath-Ammon, not to speak
of those famous places that were not of Israel, such as
Tyre and Sidon, Gath and Joppa and Ascalon as well
as Hamath and Damascus in the north.

In the later times of the Jews after the Exile Jerusalem bore a relation to the whole country that cannot
be compared simply to the position that Paris occupies
in France or London in England. It was not merely
the capital, not merely the largest city, not merely
the center of cultural influences. It stood for the
nation in a way we can understand only if we remember that most of the civilized East was organized on
the basis of a city-state. That was particularly true
of this last period when Greek influences were dominant and communities like Athens and Sparta made
their powerful claim on men's imaginations. Jerusalem
was thought of as the state proper and Judea its
supporting territory just as Athens was the heart of
Attica, and a Jew from any part of the country might
call himself a Jerusalemite when he travelled and not
be thought to misdescribe himself.

This was not the case in the dim ages when the
Jebusites held the citadel or when Solomon or Hezekiah throned in it. If Jerusalem was then used as the
symbol of the country in poetry, it was a figure of

speech.   Yet the figure of speech approached sober description when the city so far outstripped others that it became the only really great city, absorbing all the elements of national life by concentrating all the religious life in itself.   Samaria in the north may have been larger and more splendid than Jerusalem ever became at any time before the Exile, but Samaria never completely eclipsed its rivals.   Dan, Bethel, Shechem maintained themselves against their younger sister.

What were they like at their highest—Samaria under Jeroboam II, Jerusalem under Manasseh? How are we to imagine them?   About some ancient cities, those of the Greeks, scholars and archaeologists know a great deal, and their researches have become public property.   The information is in school-books.   Pictures and reconstructions abound.   Almost every educated man can to some extent visualize what a Greek city looked like in the best epoch of Greek life.   He thinks of it as a fine disposition of buildings, a gleam of distributed colors, of open spaces, of large and graceful lines.   Of course the best epoch of Greek life is the very close of the biblical period.   Athens in the days of Hezekiah was a poor little village.   Yet even the Athens of the seventh century contained the promise of its later glory.   Its colors were crude and glaring.   Its courts were straggling enclosures, its columns rude and clumsy, but the raw material was there and out of it came the artistic marvels of the days of Praxiteles.

Since an ancient city generally means to our imaginations a Greek city, we should be inclined to picture the beginnings of Jerusalem in a similar form, and its later stage as like the magnificence we can evoke from the ruins of Miletus. Unfortunately there is little justification for doing so. As far as we can be certain of such things, we can be certain that until the days of the Hellenizers, Jerusalem did not at any stage of its development look at all like a Greek city. It had no lofty buildings, no white marble colonnades, no brilliantly colored designs nor finely carved friezes. There were no monuments, no parks, no fountains, little visible ornamentation of any kind. Nothing was further from the minds of even the most sumptuous monarchs than to turn the entire city into an organized work of art. Ultimately that is what the Greeks did with their cities. The artistic genius of the Jews was not of the same sort as that of their Ionian neighbors. It took no concrete and plastic form. When we think of Jerusalem we must put out of our minds the gorgeous reconstructions which imaginative men have made for manuals of history. Jerusalem was builded as a city that is compact together, but it was not like Miletus or Ephesus or Athens.

But there is another picture that we must equally put out of our minds. Many travellers in the nineteenth century went to Palestine and Syria and brought back no very flattering picture of the appearance of a modern Oriental city. And with the curious myth of an unchanging East in mind, writers have sometimes asked us to think of the streets of Jerusalem as dirty lanes so narrow that a man walking in them might almost touch the houses on either side, and the whole city as little better than a collection of squalid hovels. The Nablus and Tiberias of fifty years ago may have been something like that, but hardly the city which, said the Lamenter, "men called the perfection of beauty, the joy of the whole earth."

One goes to Jerusalem today by train from Joppa or from Port Said on the Suez Canal. If we were to fancy a journey to Jerusalem from Joppa twenty-five hundred or three thousand years ago it would be one of a very different fashion. A stranger visiting the country on some commercial or political mission, an exile returning home, a refugee fleeing from his native land would probably have gone to that same Joppa, which we now call Jaffa and part of which looks like a thriving American town. Part of this modern Jaffa, Tel-Aviv, is a Jewish city in every respect. Not so the ancient Joppa. It was a very old site, far older than the Invasion. To the Jews of pre-exilic days it was a foreign harbor, difficult of access because it was in the hands of their bitter enemies. In the minds of many it was, even then, the jumping off place for strange adventures, expeditions to Tarshish, to the Islands and who could say to what of mysteries beyond. After the Exile it became more familiar. The men of Jerusalem as well as those of Joppa were subjects of the same foreign overlord, and the harbor—a poor enough harbor at best—became the ordinary avenue for commercial communication with the rest of the world.

We can scarcely get rid of the habit of thinking of cities in their commercial aspects, as huge fairs or bazaars, where goods of all varieties are sold. A great many cities grew up out of such fairs but that was in mediaeval times in Europe. The ancient city was rarely of such origin. Its purpose was in keeping with the wall which was its distinguishing mark. It was a place of shelter. The open countryside was essentially unsafe and, when relatively secure, it was only because of the walls of some city at no great distance.

The road that led to Jerusalem from Joppa or from anywhere else was a narrow and unpaved one. Road-building on a great scale was a Roman hobby and the Roman influence is almost wholly subsequent to biblical times. One could scarcely have convinced the ancient Israelites that many elaborate roads were necessary or desirable. For the masters of great empires, strategic roads over which armies could pass readily and swiftly were useful instruments for maintaining what the sword had won. But for the people of a small kingdom who could travel comfortably on foot from Dan to Beersheba, in less than a week, of what earthly use could they be? On the occasions of the great festal pilgrimages the absence of good roads might be keenly felt, but none of these festivals came in the thick of the rainy season, when we may suppose the roads particularly bad.

The broad roads on which wagons could pass were very few. They generally connected two important places and went straight to their destination without break or deviation. The most travelled ones had inns at various points. Itinerant merchants and beggars might station themselves by the roadside to ply their trades, especially in the festival season. On both sides in thickly populated sections—the road from Joppa to Jerusalem went through such a section—peasant huts were visible in all directions, sometimes grouped into small villages and often quite isolated. These last would now and then be on a grander scale, when they were the homes of wealthy land-owners who as likely as not had city houses as well.

Of course many of these roads were very old. But their lasting qualities were due to their frequent use and not to their construction. When the land became depopulated the first things to fall into decay were the roads, which in every revival of prosperity had to be cleared and "made straight" again until that act became a favorite metaphor with poets to express the act of spiritual reformation.

As has been stated the roads were direct lines between two places. They formed no intersecting networks. Apparently they never crossed each other. But between them there were hundreds of narrow paths which were of all conditions and of varying importance. Some were lanes between walled estates. Such doubtless was the path of the vineyards through which Balaam rode upon the ass, a path so narrow that a single armed man could bar the way to it and where a pedestrian could not turn aside without literally hugging the wall. Balaam's foot, we remember, was crushed when his ass attempted to turn aside, without advantage to the prophet's irascible temper.

What would happen in times of invasion? The high roads were at once unavailable but the by-paths would be used by the fleeing peasantry. Hence one of the first acts of devastation would be the destruction of the paths. Here again figures used in poetry must help us. The paths were "made crooked:" they were "fenced up." That is to say, they were torn up, so that the customary connection between them would be obliterated; and when they were paths like that in which Balaam rode, they were walled in at either end so as to be completely useless. The enormous importance of all these paths and roads is evidenced by the constant mention of them in poetry. They were the veins and arteries of social life. It is not too much to say that they constituted the first visible difference between the desert and the cultivated land. A wilderness was a place without paths.

But roads lead to cities and most roads in southern Palestine led to Jerusalem. We have quite lost sight of our imaginary traveller who is hurrying along the Joppa road to the great city. He has probably seen towers on his way, towers of temporary refuge for flocks and herds and small peasant villages, adequate against ordinary casual marauders. But his goal is the higher towers he can descry from a great distance, the towers that flanked the gates of the city.

For the road leads right to the city's gate which is its natural and predetermined end. There were many such gates in Jerusalem. The most simple way to name them would be, it seems to us, to call them by the name of the place to which and from which they led. That, however, was not uniformly done. We know that one of the northern gates was called the Gate of Ephraim, no doubt because it led to Samaria. Many years later we hear of the Damascus Gate, which may have been established in very ancient times. Intercourse of all sorts, often friendly enough, existed between Damascus and Jerusalem. But we also hear of the Fish Gate, the Sheep Gate, the Water Gate, the Dung Gate, the East Gate, the Old Gate, the Horse Gate, the Fountain Gate, the Valley Gate, the Corner Gate—all names which indicate that popular designations are casual and descriptive and are based on no particular system.

Even casual recollection of the Bible will bring to mind how often the word "gates" is used as the symbol of the city. They must have loomed large in the people's imaginations, these breaks in the city wall, with their portals of massive metal or wood covered with metal, the huge bars that bolted them, the tall towers on either side. Just at the gate, the wall was particularly thick—thick enough to allow of houses being built upon it. The roof of the gate was itself a broad place, where several persons could stand. Here the watcher climbed when Ahimaaz, the son of Zadok, ran to David with the news of Absalom's death and the tidings died on his lips before the ashen, suffering face of the king whom the Lord loved.

Before the gate there was an open space at which the road spread out into something like a great square. The gates were open from sunrise to sunset in times of peace, but it is not to be supposed that any one for any purpose could without more ado pass through the open portals. A stranger would be likely to stop for a while at the open space before the gates. Certainly much happened there. There foreign envoys with their suites would be received and this would make a very grand occasion. Foreign merchants who had not as yet secured a protector or patron within the city would be likely to remain there for several days, would pitch their tents on the spot and exhibit their wares; for plenty of people were certain to be about. At nightfall the gates were closed and barred, but unless raids were apprehended men might be fairly secure outside of the gates and in the dry season pass the night there quite comfortably.

In the daytime there were numbers of city folk just outside of the gates who were in fact the overflow of the throng that was just inside them. And that there was a throng just inside of them was due to a simple fact: the gate opened directly upon a market place.

There were many market places in a large city and it was quite customary for them to be directly at the gates. When we noticed the names of the gates, it must have been apparent that some of them were named from the markets which were near them. Indeed the gate was doubtless built for the market's convenience. That was certainly the case with the Sheep Gate and the Fish Gate.

But if there were several markets, there was always one market par excellence, *the* market of any city. We do not know just where the great market of Jerusalem was. We may guess reasonably enough that it was at the Old Gate or the Ephraim Gate. It was at any rate a large open space. If it resembled markets in other cities it was approximately rectangular. On all sides were the booths of merchants, mostly foreign merchants. We must not imagine that these booths resembled the shops of Greek and Roman cities. In all likelihood they were merely open tents with the merchandise spread on the ground before them and the merchant sitting gravely cross-legged on a cushion in the tent opening. The merchants were grouped by nationalities, so that the Tyrians were in one corner, the Egyptians in another, the Chaldeans in a third. In the later periods, even Gazites and Ascalonites and Edomites were to be found there, unpopular as these names always were to Jewish ears.

The people in the market place were mostly men and most of them would have been hard put to it to tell what special business brought them there. It was natural for them to be there at certain hours of the day. In this respect the life of Jerusalem was like the life of most Mediterranean cities. It was a life spent as far as practicable in the open air. Houses were places of refuge and rest and meals. They were not the centers of social life. In the market place a man met his friends, heard and discussed the news of the day, conducted his public and private business. No tocsin was necessary to call the citizens together during the market hours if it became necessary to hear a public proclamation. The crier could take his announcement to the public because he knew exactly where to find the public.

The market place was not only the business square and place of assemblage, it was also the court room. Here beneath the open sky cases were heard and adjudicated; the guilty condemned, the delinquent debtor consigned to his creditor. The procedure was simple. Every day the elders of the city might be found seated on stools, perhaps on a platform in the center of the market, for the purpose of administering justice. Whoever wished might accuse and he might accuse one of the very dignitaries before whom he appeared. Naboth for example in the dramatic incident so often mentioned in the Bible sat "on high" among the elders and nobles that fatal day on which the machinations of

Jezebel were carried out. "And there came in two men, children of Belial, and sat before him: and the men of Belial witnessed against him, even against Naboth, in the presence of the people, saying, Naboth did blaspheme God and the king." So it happened in many another case in which simpler and more humdrum matters were concerned than treasons and blasphemies and the rapacity of kings.

We may suppose that when such a proceeding was toward, the usual affairs were suspended and the Tyrian traffickers themselves crowded together with their clients to hear what was going on. And it was not merely a curious interest in another's jeopardy, which is a human if unpleasant characteristic. It was in general a very substantial security against injustice, however ineffective in the case of the unfortunate Naboth. It gave publicity to the proceedings. The spectators formed no jury and no council. Formally they were no part of the court at all. The judge or judges had sovereign jurisdiction. But evidently before a listening throng that possessed by oral transmission a good deal of the ancestral tradition it was not easily possible even for arbitrary judges to flout accepted notions of right and wrong.

And the nearness of the gate served a special purpose on such occasions. A man doomed to death—and many offenses were capital—was incontinently taken outside of the city and executed in the broad space before the gate. The same throng that witnessed his trial might be actively engaged in stoning him, if that form of punishment was involved. Between trial and execution there was no great interval in space or time. Only the gate lay between them.

But the judicial incidents of the market were not always so grim. Transactions of any sort, sales of land, of slaves, the designation of heirs—all matters that need registration or recordation in our times—were performed before these very elders in the way just indicated. Claimants to property had to keep in mind that the memories and experience of the men in the market must be reckoned with. This would not be a satisfactory system in modern commercial communities that number several millions. It worked very well for appreciably smaller communities that were in no sense commercial.

The crowd in the market was chiefly but not exclusively composed of men. Some at least of the purchasing for the household was done by women. The valorous woman of Proverbs probably bought her wool and flax and if she did, she had to go to the market to get it. Doubtless ladies of wealth and position sent their slaves to buy for them, but it is suggested that energetic housewives tended to these matters in person. Yet if women might not only with propriety, but even with commendation, be seen at the shops of the Tyrian merchants, they formed no part of the crowd that walked or sat about in the square in unreproved idleness. Such mingling of the sexes would have been highly indecorous in all ancient communities, even in those that did not put their women into actual seclusion.

But children were there in great numbers and were permitted, it seems, an almost unrestricted indulgence of their animal spirits. The "streets" which the biblical writers describe as the playground of children are certainly the markets and other squares of the city rather than the streets proper. In later times children are specifically mentioned as forming a characteristic part of the market crowd. It would certainly have been rather unnatural if they had not found their way into the center of all that was curious and exciting in the life of the city.

In a great city like Jerusalem the market activities spread beyond the confines of the public square. Streets running off it were quickly monopolized by various crafts. So there was a street of the bakers, from which Jeremiah in prison was provided with bread by royal command. In later times the goldsmiths were settled in the square near the Sheep Gate. In the same way other streets and squares might be named after some striking thing associated with them—not at all as our streets are designated now by arbitrary names which are their proper and permanent appellations, but by descriptive terms which might change if the descriptions became no longer accurate. Bakers' Street in Jerusalem would have ceased to be so called if the bakers deserted it. Baker Street in London has for many centuries harbored none of that craft, if it ever did.

The squares that were the scenes of such constant and varied human activity were not always filled. It was after all only the public life that unrolled itself there. Yet the public life of ancient communities included much that we should call social activities. In an age without newspapers, without theaters, without organized or unorganized sports, the pleasures derived from human contacts were obtained chiefly from the almost daily concourse in the market place.

But there were after all physical hindrances to continued presence in the market, besides the hindrances due to the inner and personal life which each man lived within the closely knit and compact circle of his family. East Mediterraneans might enjoy the sun but not a whole day of it. The market hours were in the morning before the noonday heat. And when on King Ahaz's great sun-dial the shadow dwindled to a little black spot, we may imagine that the crowds had long thinned out, the wares on the matting before the merchants' booths had been redeposited to safer keeping within the tents, the din and babble of eager conversation had died away. Soldiers on guard at the gates, straggling loiterers, homeless wayfarers, might still be found in the sun-lit spaces, but the great majority of the citizens were reclining on their couches in the secluded upper or lower chambers of their houses.

These houses were not far away. The portions of the city that were most removed from the market were the royal residence and the temple precincts. The houses of the mass of citizens began right at the market itself and ran on in all directions along the narrow streets that issued from it.

These streets pretended to no beauty. They were lanes between the blank walls of the houses. Chariots could pass through them but it is doubtful whether they could pass abreast. Nor were the streets paved except with irregular cobble stones. Sometimes, indeed, the bare rock on which part of the city was built might show through. If the houses on either side had been high the whole street would have been in shadow almost throughout the day. But there were few houses of more than one story. The second story, where it existed, was generally in the interior court.

Nor were the streets laid out in any set pattern. Probably there were several broad streets that cut through the city and led directly to the palace or the temple, but the majority formed simply the limits of a group of houses. The ruins of cities that have been uncovered sufficiently to enable us to gain a general view show a ground plan that is almost a maze. There were often open spots where several of the streets ran together and these spots are frequently meant when the word "streets" occurs in the Bible. In these miniature squares a certain amount of neighborly intercourse took place. Women and the smaller children of the section might foregather there with a little less impropriety than in the great market.

The impression that one might gain from Jerusalem in any of its periods would be repeated with few variations in the other cities of the country, cities that have such special association for Bible readers as Samaria, Shechem, Gibea, Jericho. It was not because these cities imitated Jerusalem, but because there was only one type for cities to conform to. Everywhere we have the walls, the gates, the markets near the gates, the clustered houses with their blank outside walls separated by narrow lanes. Probably there were many distinctions between cities due to historical accidents of growth and peculiarities of the ground on which they were built. But in general other cities differed from Jerusalem in being smaller, having fewer gates and markets and fewer great houses of powerful nobles. Samaria under Jeroboam II was more superb than its Judaic contemporary, but the post-exilic Jerusalem with its world-renowned shrine became even in the earliest waves of Greek influence a city of real magnificence. Yet except in Judea itself Jerusalem after the Exile had to admit the existence of rivals. There were other notable towns, some with shrines more ancient than the great House of the Lord on the Zion hill—so ancient that priest and prophet never completely eradicated from the minds of the Congregation of the Lord a sense of the sanctity of Dan and Bethel.

Of this great House of the Lord there is no room here to speak. With the royal palace and its surroundings it formed a very large part of the city. How the first

House was built by King Solomon with the help of
Tyrian workmen out of precious woods from Lebanon
and elsewhere, fills several chapters in the Book of
Kings. The description is full enough to make plausible restorations of the building possible. One very
elaborate restoration is to be found in a much read
History of Art by MM. Perrot and Chipiez. Pictures
of some sort are indispensable for those of us to whom
details of construction are dry and unconvincing. Even
if considerable ruins of the third Temple should be
uncovered by newer excavations, we should probably
not have to modify the pictures of the Perrot-Chipiez
history to any notable extent, since these writers were
architects as well as scholars and did their work with
fine imagination and skill. Above all, we must try to
think of the Temple in its setting and not as an isolated building. It was not a single structure but a
series of them culminating in the building that held
the inner shrine, the Holy of Holies.

This inner shrine was merely a nucleus around
which had grown a considerable number of rings within
rings. There were the treasure chambers, the houses
of the priests, of the Levites and of the numerous other
clans that conducted parts of the sacred ritual. Then
there were the side precincts set aside for the worshippers and for the visitors. And there must have
been room in which tents could be erected to house
the thousands of pilgrims that streamed here at the
seasons of the great feasts. Besides all this we must

not forget that the ritual was a sacrificial one and that it therefore implied stalls for the animals and hundreds of utensils for the various other commodities necessary to ancient worship. It could scarcely have been otherwise than a bustling, stirring place at ordinary times and contained at the great feasts a throng that only the awe of the Holy Place prevented from becoming a confused crowd.

At Delphi in Greece excavations have been so thorough that we can easily see what such a shrine of sacrifice and pilgrimage must have involved in the way of ground and buildings. The difference was that in Delphi the shrine and its surrounding structures was the whole city. In Jerusalem it was merely a portion of a populous capital.

The Temple at Jerusalem and its environs could be turned on occasion into a fort, as the tragic episodes of later history proved. But the fort proper of the city lay elsewhere. It lay in the quarter of the city in which the king lived.

The king's house was not a single structure, like palaces of modern capitals. Its models were the royal residences of Egypt and Assyria. An example of a similar system more likely to be generally familiar was the palace of the Caesars in Rome which was in point of fact a maze of buildings filling to overflowing what had once been the confines of an entire city. Or we might go to the other end of the world to gain a glimpse of the Forbidden City of Peking and find another and

still existing instance of a palace that is really a city.
The royal City of David was, we may be sure, far less
magnificent and elaborate than either the Golden
House of Nero or the Palace of Kublai Khan, but it
probably compared very favorably with the residences
of any other potentates of the ancient worlds, if we
except the Egyptian or Mesopotamian emperors.

As has already been suggested, it was in fact as well
as in name a city within the city. It had its own wall
and its own gates and the space within the wall held
a series of courts and edifices of varying sizes. In them
lived the king, his many wives, his numerous children.
Many of the wives and older children had houses of
their own with all the appurtenances of complete residences. Then there was the horde of attendants, slaves
and soldiers who ministered to the king's household.
A great many of these were high officials who lived in
houses of considerable size within the royal city. That
would be especially true of the military officials, the
captains of the king's body-guard or of his foreign
mercenaries, as well as the chiefs of his eunuchs. But
even the slaves and servants of less distinction had
houses of their own, as did the many specialized craftsmen who were needed to satisfy the wants of this
community.

Between this community and the larger city around
it there was of course constant intercourse. But it
might be said that the residents of the former came
into Jerusalem proper much more frequently than the

ordinary citizens went into the royal city. Residence
in the latter was a privilege. Those who had it were
almost self-sufficient in every respect. Even their
water supply had an independent source; so that it
was possible for the royal palace to hold out years
after the rest of the city was in the hands of the enemy.
The lower city had been in the hands of the Israelites
for generations when David finally captured the site
of his later residence. And centuries later Judah the
Maccabee took Jerusalem and the Temple, but the
foreign garrison remained in the citadel for more than
twenty years longer. The citadel in question did not
play the same part as in the ancient city. It had
ceased to be identical with the royal residence. In the
earlier days, however, citadel and palace were the same.
Royal dynasties in the ancient world were founded and
ended, quickly and suddenly. The first act of the new
master was to seize the citadel, just as he found it
safest to remain there for a considerable time and rule
his subjects from within its protecting walls. It is quite
natural, accordingly, that he should prefer to reside
there permanently.

Of other public buildings we hear little or nothing.
In ancient cities outside of Palestine there were several
temples and accordingly several edifices standing quite
apart from their surroundings and constructed in a
more splendid fashion. Even in the northern cities of
Israel, if there was a shrine it was likely to be the only
one; so that what has been said of Jerusalem is true

of all of them. But if public buildings in the real sense were lacking, the houses of the nobles partly took their place.

These nobles or elders had a real function in the community. They formed no organized senate, but common opinion and general consent easily marked out certain outstanding men of wealth and influence. We may suppose that their houses were not unlike the king's—a number of courts surrounding separate buildings, all of them contained within an enclosure. They might be built of expensive materials, adorned as elaborately as a royal residence, but they lacked altogether the citadel character which was so striking an indication of the place in which the king lived.

That the city has occupied our attention so much more fully than the country is due to our prepossessions. Our modern civilization is an urban one. It derives from the great cities of the Greek and Roman world a preoccupation with urban life that makes us think of a nation as the sum of its cities. This was not really true even for the Greeks. It was far from being true for the Jews. The majority of the people lived upon the soil, in close contact and intimate association with it. Their lives were saturated with associations of harvest and ploughing, of the wine press and the olive orchard. In the smaller cities most of the inhabitants had fields and farms within easy reach. The great cities alone were detached from the life that was in a real sense the life of the people. Except for the artisans whose services were indispensable, the great city became essentially the abode of the nobles, whose large estates lay at some distance and were administered by stewards and slaves.

No doubt a city proletariat soon came into existence, but it never became very large and played no such part in Hebrew history as did the urban mobs of Athens and Rome. It is curious that, often as the poor are mentioned in the Bible, it is the country poor that seem to be in mind, the peasant whose little field furnished him a precarious livelihood, the farm laborer who had no settled abode and lived where he could find work. Beggars, too, were beggars of the country, except at the great feasts when they must have come in throngs in the wake of the pilgrims.

The country possessed all gradations from the very rich to the poor and destitute. The city was the place of the "princes of the people," whose life was external to the main current of national existence and was felt to be the farthest departure from that which was pleasing to God.

CHAPTER VII

PERSONAL APPEARANCE

WE know what Romans looked like. Thousands of portrait busts have come down to us, in which every wrinkle and facial peculiarity of the masters of the world have been literally petrified. Of the Greeks we are not so sure in spite of the tens of thousands of Greek busts and statues and vase paintings that have survived. It is obvious that in most cases these representations show an ideal rather than a fact, but they tell us at any rate what the Greeks wished to look like and the ideal must have been based on what they saw.

So, for Egyptians and Assyrians whose countless monuments stare at us from museums and books, we can form a fairly correct image of what they looked like. These pictures are no more realistic than Greek portraits, but they preserve the general contour of the face, they indicate stature and head formation, and in the cases of the Egyptians are supplemented by the actual mummified bodies. Even of the almost vanished Hittites, the crudely carved sculptures are quite enough to enable us to imagine them in a way that cannot be very different from their appearance in the flesh.

But the Jews were commanded to make no graven images. We know that this command was variously interpreted. It was never taken to exclude vegetable or inanimate forms. And even animal representation was not wholly forbidden. Shema, the minister of Jeroboam II, used a finely carved lion as his signet ring. So did Nathaniah the son of Obadiah at about the same time. Shebaniah, the servant of King Uzziah of Judah, had a human figure on his seal that might have been meant as a portrait. Animal figures in relief are found in the synagogues of Galilee and in the Jewish cemeteries of Italy which date from the rigorous days of the first centuries of the common era. But of human figures in the form of statues or in large relief, there is no trace. If the danger of idolatry was present in any animal figure, it was imminent in human figures. The freest interpretation of the second commandment, provided it stopped short of downright repudiation, would have allowed no portrait statue or painting. We must therefore fall back on wholly different evidence if we wish to form an image of the biblical people as they seemed to their contemporaries.

The relevant passages in the Bible are few indeed. And few as they are, they play practically no part in determining our mental picture of biblical people. That picture is derived from other sources. Chiefly, I suppose, it is derived from pictures we have seen of biblical incidents, pictures that in one way or another are copies of Renaissance paintings. In these paintings, however, the faces are all the faces of contemporary Italians or else are somewhat generalized, and in any case they are not based on a supposed resemblance to the characters whom they represent.

Another way in which we imagine biblical personages is to think of them as resembling the modern Jews who are assumed to be their descendants. Something might be said for this, if it were not for the fact that our notion of what modern Jews look like is based upon tradition rather than observation. In common speech, there is a "Jewish" nose, a "Jewish" habit of body and other characters not so clearly defined. We see modern illustrators of the Bible wavering between their desire to give Abraham or Moses or David these specifically "Jewish" characteristics and the awe which tempts them to give to these sacred figures a more conventionally sacred appearance.

Unfortunately for the tradition, the most striking of these "Jewish" characteristics, the nose, is not Jewish at all. Most Jews do not have it and other national groups have it more commonly than Jews. Among these groups are the Armenians, and by a combination of several guesses, it has come to be generally believed that the modern Armenians are the descendants of the ancient Hittites. Whether we shall continue to think so as we make greater progress in deciphering the Hittite inscriptions is doubtful, but the opinion has a certain currency at present.

Now the Hittite monuments show a great many sculptured figures most of whom have a markedly aquiline or "Jewish" nose. And the Hittites certainly occupied Palestine in pre-biblical times as well as much of the surrounding country. On the collapse of their great empire individual Hittites seem to have been absorbed into the various nations of Palestine and Syria. Uriah, the unfortunate rival of David, shows that Hittites were still distinct as a group, but lived side by side with the Jews as worshippers of the same God and intermarrying with them. A few centuries later the prophet flings in the face of an arrogant Judah its Hittite mother and its Amorite father. So, if the Hittite nose is the "Jewish" nose, it can readily have come into the inheritance of the Jews from this Hittite strain.

But it ought to be apparent from the foregoing that all of this depends on a series of guesses. If we were forced to rely wholly upon the appearance of modern Jews in order to form our picture of ancient Jews, we should have to fancy their lineaments as exhibiting almost every conceivable contour and shape. And it would be very nearly the same if we were to depend upon the appearance of modern Palestinians and Arabs. All varieties of facial appearance are found among them and few of the physical traits are the typically "Semite" or "Jewish" ones. Of course invasion and immigration have introduced a great many racial strains into these countries, but that merely makes our problem the more difficult.

If it is practically impossible to imagine the nose and head form of ancient Jews and ancient Palestinians except by guessing, we are on a little better ground as to their color. We have reason to suppose that most of them were dark. It ought hardly to be necessary to add that the hue of their skin was not due to the fact that they lived in a warm climate and were habitually sunburnt. To discuss the bearing of this on the question before us would involve us in a profoundly difficult biological question which is now again agitating scientists. A better reason for coming to the above conclusion is that the present inhabitants of the desert, as well as of Palestine, are quite generally dark-skinned and black-haired. There is a certain percentage of fair-haired and light-skinned people among them but it is not large enough to change the general impression.

But it is still more to our purpose that there are at least a few biblical references to the fact. The Bible does not say anything whatever about the faces or heads of the people it mentions, but it does sometimes refer to their color. The lover surely, and the beloved perhaps, of the Song of Songs call each other *shahor*, which the translations render by "black" or "swarthy." "I am black but comely, O ye daughters of Jerusalem," runs the song, "as the tents of Kedar, as the curtains of Solomon. Look not upon me because I am black, because the sun has looked upon me." And again the Bride says, "His locks are bushy and black as a raven."

The tents of Kedar used here for purposes of comparison are the tents of the nomad Bedouin to this day. The word *shahor* is also used of black horses and black goats' hair, so there is no doubt what the word means. As far as the hair is concerned, it is "black as a raven," a comparison as current and proverbial then as it is now.

These love songs that are collected in the Song of Songs are in the Oriental manner. Many of their similes cannot possibly be meant literally. But if this one is not meant literally, there seems little point in using it. It may, to be sure, represent an ideal as well. The reference to the lover's dark color would scarcely be repeated unless that color was supposed to be something particularly beautiful. The only question is whether we may draw the inference that what was particularly beautiful was the best example of what was relatively common. It seems a plausible supposition. In that case we should think of most of the actors in the biblical story as black-haired and quite noticeably dark-hued—somewhat like the inhabitants of modern Palestine, or like southern Spaniards or Italians.

Between this dark skin and "black" as we understand it, there was a sharp contrast. The Ethiopians, for example, were black and there were a number of Ethiopians in Palestine. Most of those particularly mentioned were slaves or menials, but that implied no repugnance or abhorrence. On the contrary, at least one line of tradition tells us of an Ethiopian wife of Moses and later rabbinic legend made of Ebed-Melech, the Ethiopian who rescued Jeremiah, something of a national saint. When an Ethiopian king sat on the crumbling throne of Pharaoh and sent armies to Syria to ward off impending doom from Israel and Judah, Ethiopia became one of the great and distant empires upon which the power of the Lord would be exhibited. At that time surely some Ethiopians must have been persons of note in Palestine and not strange and repulsive barbarians.

But even then they were sharply marked out in color from the rest of the population. The famous phrase of Jeremiah shows that: "Can the Ethiopian change his skin or the leopard his spots?" The swartness or blackness of the lovers in Canticles must therefore be a color quite different from that of the Ethiopians and not merely a slightly lighter hue.

We have assumed on the evidence of the Song of Songs that dark skin was, if anything, preferred by lovers, and have drawn the inference that such a color was common. We might indeed have drawn the opposite inference. Greek poets speak of golden-haired or tawny-haired gods and heroes, and it is often asserted that this proves such a color to have been rare and a mark of high birth, while dark hair was the sign of the common man. We might therefore on this basis say the opposite for Judea, that the Bridegroom and Bride of Canticles represent the ideal type of beauty, a necessarily rare thing, and that therefore the mass of the inhabitants were tawny or blond. I should not like to maintain this paradox in detail, but that a certain number of Jews were fair or red or tawny in hair and coloring is highly probable. Edom, Israel's kinsman, was named for his redness, although scholars are not agreed as to what that "redness" was.

No person in the Bible is unmistakably referred to as having blond hair or a fair complexion. Of David it is said that he was "ruddy and withal of a beautiful countenance," and again we read that Goliath disdained David, "for he was but a youth and ruddy and of fair countenance." It is conceivable, but very unlikely, that "ruddy" means "light-haired" or "red-haired" in this connection, a fact of no great moment since it is certainly probable enough on general grounds that there was a sprinkling of blond and light-skinned people among the inhabitants of the country. But some silly persons in modern times have seized eagerly upon the statement to prove that David was an Aryan or a Nordic or what not. A good deal of solemn nonsense has been written on the subject — nonsense scarcely deserving refutation.

As a matter of fact the Nazirites are called "ruddy" in the Book of Lamentations and it will scarcely be urged that the word means blond or fair-haired in this passage. And again the very Bridegroom who so emphatically calls himself "black," is called "white and ruddy" by his beloved in almost the same breath in which she says that "his locks are black as a raven."

The natural interpretation of the words would refer them to the fresh glow of vigorous health in all these

cases. The context of the references to David shows
this, even without the confirmation of other passages.
We may be sure that no other interpretation would
ever have been put upon the words, had not romantic
propagandists in the nineteenth century felt themselves constrained to harmonize their racial supercili-
ousness with their foreign religion.

The size and stature of the biblical men we must
also guess at. The Bible tells us little about it. There
was a tradition which persisted for many centuries that
the invading Covenanters had dispossessed a race of
very tall men, the Emim and the Anakim, especially
the latter. These "giants," as they are sometimes
called, may have deserved their name only by comparison with the average of their neighbors. Real giants
measured by nursery rhyme standards they certainly
were not. In any case, the tradition seems to prove
that the Israelites were not exceptionally tall men and
in that respect were probably like other Canaanites.
Just so the Romans seemed small of stature in comparison with the Northern races, although they were
quite the equals of the other Mediterranean nations.

Bodily strength, grace of form and movement, were
strong recommendations in Israel as elsewhere. War-
fare in ancient times was largely a matter of individual
hand to hand encounters and the prowess of famous
leaders had to be demonstrated visibly over and over
again. The heroic companions of David whose valor is
recounted at the close of the second book of Samuel

were men of great physical strength as well as skill and courage and devoted loyalty—Adino, Eleazar, Shammah, the redoubtable sons of Zeruiah, and especially Benaiah, who imitated his master by slaying a lion in a pit as well as lion-like men.

So much we might well expect, but one characteristic is often mentioned which we do not ordinarily associate with courage and strength, namely, fleetness of foot. The lament over Saul and Jonathan says that they were "swifter than eagles, stronger than lions." The speed of Ahimaaz is mentioned as a trait of merit. Asahel, brother of Joab, outran to his sorrow even the swift Abner. We can scarcely be surprised at this, however, when we remember Homer's fleet heroes, especially the foremost of all of them, Achilles, who was not more emphatically the strongest than he was the quickest of his associates. And Abner and Jonathan were, we must remember, quite literally contemporaries of Achilles. For that reason the relative scarcity of horses and chariots cannot be the reason for this exaltation of fleetness, since the Homeric heroes had horses and chariots in plenty. And even horses and chariots were of use principally on the way to the actual battlefield, and a warrior to be effective had a great deal of fighting to do where horses and chariots were useless. We can see that apart from the esteem shown to any form of bodily power, rapidity of movement would be of signal advantage where one man faced odds, as the best known warriors were apt to do.

People who lived largely in the open, even when they lived in the city and who, when they lived in the country, were husbandmen and mountain herdsmen, could scarcely fail to be possessed of wiry and hard bodies. As the Orientals are to this day, so probably the Israelites were erect in bearing with a good deal of natural dignity. From what has been said the only thing we can call even a plausible guess about their appearance is that most of them were dark and of medium stature. To fill out the rest of the picture, we must depend wholly upon our imaginations.

CHAPTER VIII

DRESS AND ORNAMENTS

THOSE who are interested in such matters can readily discover in unimpeachable records the enormous proportion of our national wealth that is in some form invested in clothes. The shops of any city, large or small, certainly seem filled to a disproportionate extent with clothes or materials for clothes. Further, popular belief has credited Jews with a large share in the administration of this economic and social factor of our community.

It will hardly be supposed by any one that biblical men and women were as much absorbed in this element of their external lives as we are. But our record which is silent on a great deal that we should like to hear has not a little to say of dress. "Ye daughters of Israel," runs the splendid Song of the Bow, "weep over Saul who clothed you with scarlet, with other delights." And in that still older paean, the Song of Deborah, it is Sisera himself who, his women-folk exultingly hope, will find as his chief booty, "divers colors of needlework on both sides, meet for the necks of them that take the spoil." So, too, Jacob in the well known story knows no more certain way of distinguishing his favorite son than by a "coat of many colours;" and Aaron's sons are to be provided with coats "for glory and for beauty." Evidently what a man or woman put about his body had other purposes than merely to keep the cold away.

That one of the least noble of these purposes is the mere ostentation of wealth, we shall not be able to deny either for the biblical people or for any other people. And as among all other nations, this ostentation has been the most obvious target for the attacks of reformers and moralists. Laws limiting the quality, the style, the cost of clothing were frequently passed in Greek and Roman communities, generally with as little success as such sumptuary legislation has met with in later times. But except for one curious prohibition, sumptuary laws do not seem to have been issued by the Hebrews. The minute regulations of attire which occupy so much space in Leviticus are concerned with the priests whose clothing must of course partake of the ritual purity of their persons. All the more do the prophets who denounce the pride that is the besetting sin of the powerful, use as symbols of that pride the "broidered work, the silk, the fine linen," in which visible proofs of wealth the proud man stalked among his humbler fellows.

Ancient sumptuary legislation is often specifically directed against the dress of women. Women were credited in ancient times with an interest in ornament and dress that amounted to a passion—with what justice we cannot tell. If it was true, there is much to explain it. They were excluded from most of what made men's lives active and interesting and were thus forced into an attention to house and clothing that seemed excessive to their lords. This is the usual apology for women, but it may be doubted whether an apology is necessary. Even the few illustrations already given indicate that fine raiment was not indifferent to their lords.

It is highly probable that feminine absorption in dress is in part a conventional masculine theory. It is, we must remember, a male prophet, Jeremiah, who says, "Can a maid forget her ornaments or a bride her attire?" If the prophetess Huldah as well as her great contemporary had left us her book, who knows but that the same thing might be assigned to men as the highest summit of their desires? Achan, the troubler of Israel, troubled her for the sake of a Babylonish garment, and, if the prophets are to be credited, later Achans were even more readily tempted without meeting his fate. Perhaps the forms of attire that men desired to make themselves as glorious and beautiful as Aaron's sons were different from those that women coveted, and this may account for much masculine contempt of female vanity in ancient times as well as modern.

There is probably nothing in Manners and Customs that changes so frequently as fashions of dress, a proverbial reflection that we can verify by going back ever so little in our own memories. If we add to our own the artificial memory of books the changes are almost revolutionary, and yet one striking fact of modern dress, a marked differentiation of the sexes, is of relatively recent origin. A differentiation that was striking enough to contemporary eyes always existed, but when we see ancient robes we are not always immediately sure whether they were meant for men or for women. That is, at any rate, true in the case of the ancient nations we have most in mind, the Greeks, the Romans and the Jews, and is particularly true of their festival garb. Indeed in those periods and places in the ancient world where the difference between the dress of men and women was very marked, it has often resolved itself into the fact that men frequently went unclad or partly clad and women almost never did so.

The only satisfactory way of visualizing Jewish dress to ourselves is to look at pictures, and pictures of biblical costume are just what we cannot get. Luckily we can get pictures of the dress of some of their neighbors, and that, coupled with the statements of the Bible, will amply suffice. Our chief difficulty is the usual one that no one of the many Hebrew words for parts of raiment really corresponds to anything we wear now. To this is added the fact that our translation uses the same words, cloak or coat or mantle or skirt, for a variety of articles. In some cases we shall have to use the Hebrew terms and arbitrarily identify them with certain English ones.

We may say that there were two main garments, an outer garment, the mantle, *simlah* in Hebrew, and an inner garment, the tunic, *kuttonet*. In its simplest form the latter was a sleeveless shirt with apertures for head and arms. It was worn next to the skin and reached to the knees. About this one cast the *simlah*, a great rectangular piece of cloth which could be wound around the body in a number of ways. If to these two we add the *ezor*, a broad girdle worn beneath the tunic, and the *hagor*, a belt worn outside of it, and if we picture sandals of wood or leather tied to the feet with thongs, we have the complete ordinary dress of ordinary men.

Indeed, even this simple vesture was much too elaborate for use on all occasions or in all places. Practically every man within doors and peasants and artisans out of doors wore neither sandals nor external belt nor mantle. When the Bible speaks of a man as "naked" it often means that he is clad merely in this indoor garb. But for certain labors even the tunic was discarded. Obviously this meant complete nudity except for the girdle about the loins. This was considered a mark of primitive manners and was somewhat affected by the earlier prophets as a protest against luxury and ostentation. When Elijah ran before Ahab he was so clad, except for a rude cloak which was, however, not the *simlah*.

On festal occasions a great deal more was added. Nine or ten different kinds of clothing, the character of which we can only conjecture, are mentioned in the Bible, and nearly all of them are festal garments. Yet what was a festal garment for the common man was the ordinary dress of princes and priests. The latter, particularly, when they became a sacerdotal and privileged caste, soon surpassed all other classes in the elaborateness and splendor of their dress, and contrasted sharply with the stark simplicity of the prophetic attire. Every ordinary garment here became something sumptuous. The tunic reached to the ankles. It was no longer sleeveless but had long sleeves that extended to the wrists. Over it a second tunic was placed with long flowing fringes. Upon this came the *ephod*, a sort of double chasuble, fastened at the shoulders. The inner girdle was replaced by an elaborate linen undergarment ending in trousers. It need scarcely be said that these garments were never simple but splendidly embroidered and gorgeously ornamented.

This complicated priestly apparel was in the days of Israel's prosperity emulated by princes and nobles, and at a greater distance, by the rank and file of the citizenry on special occasions. Some of the elements of priestly apparel had a ritual purpose, such as the *ephod*, the linen underclothes. It is not likely that even kings would wish to wear them. For the upper classes the distinction lay in the multiplicity of the ordinary garments, in the ornamentation, their varied cut, their costly material.

The dress of women was different in detail rather than in kind. They too wore tunic and cloak. We may suppose that in every case their dress was a little more elaborate. Doubtless they wore longer tunics, larger mantles than their men-folk. And if they did, they may be said to have had every right to them, for they generally made not only their own clothes but those of their lords.

Nothing has been said of hats. The reason is simple. Hats, as we understand them, did not exist. That is to say, a covering for the head was no part of ordinary dress. It is likely that in sudden emergencies, an unexpected rainfall or the like, a man protected his head by flinging part of his cloak over it, but the act of covering the head so often mentioned in the Bible is regularly a sign of mourning or humiliation, not a means of protection from the inclemency of the weather.

But if hats were not worn, headgear was, and by headgear I mean adornments for the head, which varied from simple bands or fillets to elaborate turbans, which again may have had several layers. The priestly miter and the royal crown were specialized forms of such headgear, and the varieties that were worn by other classes had the same purpose. They were marks of honor. Their chief function was that of ornament.

Just as there were two garments, there were two materials, linen and wool. Both of these materials had been in use in that region from a time too ancient to admit of being approximately fixed, and throughout biblical times they continue to be almost the sole textile materials. As to a knowledge of others, the evidence is dubious and dispute among scholars runs high. Silk and cotton were known in India and China in very remote antiquity. There would have been nothing impossible in pieces of such fabrics finding their way into our East Mediterranean region.

The actual manufacture of silk and cotton we know to have come quite late, much later than biblical times, so that if a few examples of silk or cotton cloth were really imported into Palestine, these stuffs could never have had any economic importance. They must have seemed exotic rarities, costly perhaps for their very rarity. We must remember, however, that it is very doubtful whether they were known at all, even in this qualified sense. The words which some scholars believe to refer to silk and cotton are of doubtful meaning. That seems to be true for the Babylonian inscriptions as well as for our Bible. In any case it will scarcely be denied that to the man of the Bible, stuff for raiment suggested either linen or wool and ordinarily suggested nothing else.

Within this relative uniformity of material there was abundant scope for differences of quality. Threads of linen or of wool are fine or coarse, selected or casually picked, dyed with elaborate colors or left in their natural state. That gives us an extensive scale, and gradations were in all probability more readily recognized than they are now, so that the contrast between fine and poor clothing was at least as apparent as it is today.

Garments made of one kind of thread only—except in the case of the cheapest material, cotton—are relatively rare at the present time. Most fabrics are mixtures. It is curious that this practice of mixing threads is explicitly forbidden in both Leviticus and Deuteronomy. "Thou shalt not wear a garment of divers sorts, as of linen and woolen together," says Deuteronomy. The prohibition of mixtures, of *shaatnez*, occurs in a group of very similar injunctions such as that of sowing the same furrow with divers seeds. It is quite inexplicable from any practical point of view. Mediaeval commentators conjectured that *shaatnez* might have been used by the neighboring heathen for some religious ceremonies. That would be quite enough to make it forbidden to Jews. But it may well be that a more primitive idea lies behind it.

Even the very poorest, accordingly, wore "all wool" or pure linen clothes. The differences between ordinary linen and fine linen seemed doubtless greater than that which we find between silk and cotton. And in wool too, there were all the varieties from the finest lamb's wool to the coarse goats' hair or camels' hair from which the scanty clothing of slaves and prophets was made.

It may be that the sackcloth so often mentioned in the Bible means a girdle of black goats' hair. If this were the common garb of the very poorest it would be natural that in an effort at self-humiliation kings and nobles should strip off their sumptuous apparel and don this dress of the lowest of their subjects. Other explanations are advanced for the use of sackcloth as the dress of mourning, and they may be just as good. But as to the nature of sackcloth there is practical agreement among learned men.

Sackcloth, of course, refers merely to the material. Instead of a girdle of sackcloth, one might have a cloak of it used like any other cloak and serving, like the girdle, a penitential purpose for those whose ordinary dress was something better.

If the supposition to which we have referred is true, and sackcloth was the common dress of the poor, their clothes would form the only quite dark spots in the picture a full market place would have presented. The rest of the picture was very different. Instead of a general aspect of soberness which crowded streets give us now, there was a constant flash of bright colors— glistening white, warm scarlets, rich blues and purples. These were the best known and most widely used dyes, since yellow and green are practically never mentioned as colors of clothing. Scarlet or red was probably most common. We must not forget, however, that words for colors are likely to be rather vague and that anything from a bright scarlet to a deep purple might be called by the name of one of the hues that happened to strike the observer. Yet even if scarlet was fairly common, it was a mark of wealth and some of the shades, especially those verging on purple, were particularly costly. So, too, was white, which must not be confounded with the color of wool or linen in its untreated state. Priests' robes in some of the most impressive functions were brilliantly white as was the garment of the Ancient of Days seen in Daniel's vision.

In scarlet, purple or white, the borders of his dress embroidered in gold and blue, the noble of Jerusalem or Samaria must have been a resplendent figure. And he becomes still more resplendent if we think of his ornaments. He wore chains about his neck, rings on his fingers, bracelets about his wrists and fillets around his head. The plural is used, for he seems to have worn tiers of these ornaments and the prouder and haughtier he was, the heavier and more complicated his encircling gold and silver decorations.

In this matter of ornament, the ladies far excelled their lords. The haughty daughters of Zion who walked with outstretched necks and mincing gait were fearful and wonderful creatures to behold, if the outraged prophet means us to think of all he enumerates as the ornaments of a single person. "In that day," he cries, "the Lord will take away the bravery of their anklets, and the fillets, and the crescents; the pendants and the bracelets and the veils; the headtires, and the armlets, and the sashes, and the corselets, and the amulets; the rings and the nose-jewels; the aprons and the mantelets, and the cloaks, and the girdles; and the

gauze robes, and the fine linen, and the turbans, and
the mantles." Many of these words are mere guesses,
ancient or modern, as to the meaning of the Hebrew
words. Masculine annotators and translators spent
little time in trying to familiarize themselves with the
corresponding details of contemporary female attire,
but were content with vague words that described
nothing in particular except the fact that women wore
many ornaments, of which they were inordinately
fond. Yet if the enumeration is even partly accurate,
the old woman of Banbury Cross was a drab and
commonplace creature beside a Judean princess in the
days of Hezekiah, and it is surprising, not that she
walked with a mincing gait, but that she walked at all.

The astounding catalogue that the prophet put together contained, we might suppose, everything that
male or female vanity could desire. It is hard to see
what can have been omitted. For some of these articles
there was better warrant than the imitation of wealthy
heathen. Earrings at least had patriarchal examples.
Rebekah wore them and so did the mystic bride of
God in the early Exile. The cheeks of the beloved in
Canticles were comely with rows of jewels and her
forehead, too, may have been so adorned. The setting
of these jewels was gold—the wrought gold of the
psalms.

Earrings were worn only by women and, it seems,
by children of either sex. "Break off the golden earrings," Aaron tells the Israelites at the foot of Sinai,

"which are in the ears of your wives, of your sons and of your daughters and bring them unto me." Men did not wear them, except the desert nomads, the Ishmaelites, of whose attire they seem to have been a striking feature. Doubtless they appeared to the Canaanites as outlandish and barbarous articles for men to wear, much as they seem to us now when we see them in the ears of Maltese sailors or Italian peasants. But if the Ishmaelites whom Gideon's men destroyed wore them, we can scarcely doubt that the Covenanters wore them too when they first crossed the Jordan and discarded them only later along with other desert customs.

Who the craftsmen were who fashioned these things we are not told. They may have come at first from abroad, from Egypt, from Phoenicia, or the Aegean islands. But there must soon have been native artists and their achievements were of a high order. Indeed ancient workmanship in these matters is particularly exquisite—quite unrivalled by anything in modern times. There was a wide range of designs that still kept within the Second Commandment, so that artistic impulses restrained in other fields by ritual prohibition may have found free rein here.

But we must not forget that the word which appears as "jewels" in our translation often refers to small objects of silver and gold and not to precious stones at all. These last were known and highly valued but they were not used quite as we use them. Precious

stones as well as gold, Solomon's guest brings from
Sheba and his ally brings from Ophir, but they seem
to have been designed to decorate crowns, caskets,
hangings, coverings or robes rather than to be placed
directly upon the hands or face, even in a gold or
silver setting.

They may even have been collected as loose stones
and treasured for their beauty and costliness without
being fixed into any other object. Most of the stones
we have were known in biblical times and, as at present, considered the standard of highest value. Only
a few were found in Palestine. Most of them were
brought there from the remotest parts of Asia and
Africa, where indeed we still seek them. Rubies,
emeralds, topazes, sapphires, diamonds, show in their
very names their Eastern origin and still continue to
exercise their strange fascination upon us. Both of
the Woman of Valour and of Wisdom, it is said that
their price was above rubies. We have retained this
means of comparison for things we value, not merely
as a biblical reminiscence, but because we still regard
these glittering pieces of stone as the most intrinsically
precious of objects.

It very soon came to be believed in Europe and Asia
that these stones had other properties than their sheer
beauty and costliness. They were credited with virtues
and powers which made them mystic or magical, and
European folklore is full of references to this fact.
Whether biblical people held this view is not quite

certain but it may well have been current among the masses and it is not impossible that the twelve stones in the High Priest's *ephod* owe their presence there to a belief in their strange and mysterious efficacy. The stone engraved with a man's name or mark and used as his signet easily became connected with him as something more intimate than a mere valuable possession. We can readily see how diamonds and topazes appeared to contain imprisoned fires which a lively imagination could turn into potent spiritual beings.

One other form of adornment is left and that is paint. Almost everything in ancient times was colored to make it appear more beautiful. This applies to precious stones, to furniture, to houses, to clothing and finally to the human body. And the painting was not a mere delicate touching with rouge but a bold application of strong tints. Common as it became it was still a foreign and not very reputable custom. Yet the highest ladies in the land resorted to it, as on the eminent occasion when the wicked Jezebel went to her certain death in what we must own was a royal and intrepid fashion. Whether they painted their entire faces or merely their eyes is not quite clear. In either case, it was frequently done to excess, until the painting made deep furrows in the skin and invited the taunts rather than the admiration of ungallant observers. To the prophets this practice of painting was the particular symbol of viciousness and they denounced it with especial vehemence.

Paint was used only by women, but perfumes were common to both sexes. Yet these perfumes, frankincense, cassia, aloes, were sprinkled, one gathers, on the robes rather than on the person. "All thy garments," says the song of loves which we call Psalm 45, "smell of myrrh and aloes and cassia out of ivory palaces." Yet the fingers of the Beloved in Canticles "drip with myrrh," and that, it seems, in a literal rather than a figurative sense. Perfumes were therefore used upon the body also but in the form of ointments. Unguents made of olive oil and aromatic spices were in constant use as indispensable parts of the daily toilet. To omit this anointing was a sign of mourning. It was resumed as soon as mourning was over. We may conjecture that to some extent these unguents took the place of soap, except that soaps of such precious materials would today be the luxury of very rich men. Yet we must observe a very important qualification in this statement. Ointments and perfumes did not become in Palestine, as they did in Renaissance Europe, a substitute for bodily cleanliness. Baths and ablutions were frequent and were actually required as a religious duty in a number of cases. Unguents were used after washing and not before and their avowed purpose was to make the person sweet-scented. "Ointment and perfume," says Proverbs, "rejoice the heart."

We do not gather that dress and toilet occupied a large part of a woman's or a man's day. The fine ladies denounced by the prophet obviously could not have bedecked themselves alone or speedily, but they had slaves and tiring women in plenty. For the others, dress was a simple matter, and it remained so even on festal occasions when the better cloak marked the better day. A certain delight in dress existed in all classes, particularly delight in the colors which dress exhibited. Perhaps, as in the case of jewels, artistic impulses thwarted in other directions expressed themselves here. But even so the work most prized was probably of foreign origin. With the Egyptian empire across the Red Sea, with the great markets of Tyre and Sidon at their borders, the Israelites would scarcely have developed the arts of luxury even if their constantly jeopardized little state had given them generations of leisure. The creative minds among them were drawn to a different form of expression, to the poetry and music which lent themselves to the special and peculiar religious organization of the Jews. Their God, after all, possessed His people in a way quite different from that in which Amon ruled Thebes or Marduk, Babylon.

CHAPTER IX

OCCUPATIONS

How the father of mankind and the mother of all living spent their long days in Eden is not told us in the legends that fill the earlier chapters of Genesis. Devout imaginations have endeavored to picture this felicity in detail. More than that, great poets have added their touches to the narrative; but apparently even Milton can find nothing else for the first couple to do than prune the luxuriant overgrowth of the garden each day, only to find the rank herbs have sprung up again during the night. One dares to guess that they were bored.

Now the regaining of Eden, in another life if not in this one, came to be in post-biblical times the dream of every Jew and through Christianity has become the avowed purpose of most Europeans and Americans. But there is nothing to show that biblical men dreamed of such a fulfilment, however remote. They had a definite picture of a Golden Age, of a life that everybody would like to lead, but it was very differently constituted from the Miltonic conception of Eden.

We shall understand their ideal if we contrast it with another one better known because stated in the terms of Greek literature and mythology. The Greeks and those Romans whose minds were Greek imagined a Golden Age very much like that of the modern Christian vision of Paradise. It is described in the archaic verses of Hesiod and eight centuries later Vergil and Horace repeat the song. Grapes and olives will grow on every vine; spikenard on every bush; unherded and unwatched flocks will come uncalled to the milking troughs. And amidst these opulent gifts of nature the Greek thought of moving like a faun or wood nymph, piping sweet strains or aimlessly reclining by the banks of purling streams. It is a gracious picture, but it is evident that the human nervous structure is not fully adapted for enjoying it.

The modern ideal is, I should say, characteristically different. Perhaps every one of the thirty million Americans now engaged in "gainful occupations" dreams of a time or a situation when without exertion on his part, he will be in receipt of a steady income of money from one of many existing sources, so that all his wants will be gratified upon pushing an electric button. He has in mind an economic organization as delicate in its mechanism as a fine watch, with thousands of interlocking cogs and wheels, and this mechanism he can only with difficulty imagine to be absent.

If we look at the biblical picture of a Golden Age, we shall find it different from either of these. A very ancient prophet, older even than Isaiah, chants it in exquisite poetry. "It shall come to pass that the mountain of the Lord's house shall be established in the top of the mountains.... But they shall sit every man under his vine and under his fig tree and **none** shall make them afraid." And almost the last of the prophets, Zechariah, repeats the thought. "But now I will not be unto the remnant of this people as in the former days, saith the Lord of Hosts. For there shall be the seed of peace; the vine shall give her fruit and the ground shall give her increase and the heavens shall give their dew." That is to say, the Hebrew thought of sitting at the end of a day, laborious but not toilsome, under trees emphatically his own, the fruit of his planting, his household and friends secure about him, we may suppose; for, says the prophet, he is to call his neighbors to him. The idyllic happiness of the scene is just this undisturbed possession of a small corner of the earth adequate to a man's needs, but adequate only by the application of a day's labor. In this respect it is not unlike the Roman picture of the carefree husbandman plowing his ancestral acres with his own oxen.

If the modern ideal, the Greek ideal and the Hebrew have anything in common it is the freedom from economic anxieties. But here they diverge. The leisure looked forward to by the modern man is possible only if highly differentiated groups of workmen and tradesmen, laborers and directors, maintain their activities much as they do at present. But neither Hebrew nor Greek demanded that some should hew wood in order that others might be relieved of this disagreeable task. Conceivably, if not probably, every family group on earth might share Hesiod's or Isaiah's imagined felicity. They knew nothing of inexorable economic laws. They would not have believed that there was a limit to the copious liberality of the earth or that there ever could be a general problem of population. If population pressed upon subsistence at any one place men might go elsewhere, there was plenty of room.

We see at once that the special significance of these pictures of a Golden Age lies in the fact that they are idealized representations of actual conditions. The family group, secure on its own fields, was not merely the ideal of a distant and irrecoverable past. It was realizable as a present possibility almost anywhere between Dan and Beersheba, if it were not for war or plague or pestilence. That is why peace was the basis of the picture. "Neither shall they (the nations)learn war any more." "There shall be the seed of peace." If the abhorred business of bloodshed could be done away with, the ordinary business of mankind could be carried on readily enough.

What was the ordinary business? If we say it was agriculture, we may create a false impression. Agriculture is the basis of modern economic life as well as of ancient, but in a vastly more limited sense. We have made of it the special occupation of a special class, as distinct as miners, carpenters, physicians. The life of the Hebrews, as we find it mirrored in all the ancient codes, was much more like that of the mediaeval villa. The unit was a family of husbandmen, a tiny community in itself, which by the efforts of its members made or grew or provided on its own soil all that it needed.

As we shall see, a specialization of functions in society had already taken place, but it was not very far advanced and it was not thought to be something desirable in itself. A man of today, for all our enormous technical achievements as a people, would as an individual have seemed a poor and helpless creature in the ancient world. Left to himself, he can do very little. He is dependent on highly trained specialists who provide him ready-made most of the materials of his livelihood. He is generally himself one of those specialists, quite incompetent out of his field. If a modern family of some size were left alone in a new land, they would probably sink to one of the earliest levels of society. A biblical household would soon have established a fair semblance of civilized comfort.

In the Bible, society was believed to be at its best when it consisted of a number of independent and self-sufficient peasant families. The two great codes of the Pentateuch and the fragments of other codes scattered throughout the Bible, assume that they are legislating for husbandmen. The man with his sons, his slaves, his alien clients and his women, plows and sows and reaps, feeds and waters his herds and shears his sheep. Whatever else he does is with materials he has procured in this way. If he is poor, his herds will be a few sheep and goats and not lordly cattle. If he is wealthy, field is added to field and the estate becomes a principality. But the essential character is the same. He lives upon the soil and his efforts and the efforts of those who belong to him are engrossed with the soil. It is not only that this is the most honored and most ancient of occupations. It is taken for granted that under normal circumstances it will be everybody's occupation and that if a man is temporarily prevented from engaging in it, he seeks to come back to it as soon as possible.

And yet in all this we have a reflection of Canaanite feeling rather than of that of the Covenanters who formed the core of the biblical people and were the source of their spiritual development. To the Covenanters, agriculture was subsidiary and of secondary importance. They were above all herdsmen of sheep and cattle. The occupation pleasing to the Lord beyond all others, therefore, was that of a shepherd. The legend of Cain and Abel is partly based on this belief and it remained in the lively recollection of song and tradition long after the people as a whole had as a matter of practical fact forgotten the nomadic habits of their ancestors. "And it shall come to pass when Pharaoh shall call you and shall say, What is your occupation? That ye shall say, Thy servants' trade hath been about cattle from our youth even until now, both we and also our fathers." Thus Joseph is made to declare to his brethren in the oldest portion of Genesis. Yet in spite of this tradition the influence of

Canaan was too strong. Following the furrow, a task hardly befitting the desert warrior, became the ideal of his children. It may be that they retained a slight predilection for the stock-raising part of agriculture. The frequent use of metaphors derived from herding indicates this. But the Israelites soon grew so rooted to the soil that the landless occupations came to have for them the stigma of an inferior order. If the desert was their mother, the pleasant land flowing with milk and honey had become their indulgent foster-mother and completely stolen their hearts.

First of all and most directly she gave them an assured food supply. At the present time our daily bread is furnished to us by an intricately organized network of farmers, millers, refiners, transporters, jobbers and retailers. Almost nothing of this existed in Palestine. Those who grew the grain, who gathered it, threshed it and winnowed it, were also the ones who ground it into flour and baked it into loaves. At any rate the process was superintended by the same persons, even if details of it were at various times assigned to various participants. Except for the fact that what is now done by steam or gasoline driven machines was then done by hand, the actual cultivation of the soil has not changed. Our imagination can follow the farmer in his sowing and reaping. Generally, however, our imagination stops there and has merely a vague knowledge that after the grains are shucked from the ear, they somehow reach us as a white flour from the grocer. That intervening process was of necessity completely familiar to every one in biblical times. Mills were not great edifices somewhere in the north of the country, but small contrivances manipulated by hand. A "mill" consisted simply of two round stones, an upper and a lower. The upper one, the "rider," fitted into the lower much as in the old-fashioned hand coffee mill the upper iron cap fits into a similarly shaped contrivance beneath it.

Primitive as this method was, there was an even ruder way of grinding corn. The garnered grains might be placed in a small earthenware pot or mortar and then beaten and bruised and ground with a wooden pestle until the husk was completely separated from the kernel. This older method was especially used for the offerings of the first fruits. "If thou offer a meat offering of thy first fruits unto the Lord," says Leviticus, "thou shalt offer . . . . . green ears of corn dried by the fire, even corn beaten out of full ears." This is precisely what we might expect in religious practices. Instruments discarded in ordinary life, such as flint knives, were retained for ritual purposes among both Romans and Jews. There was always the feeling that the ritual could not safely be changed even in minute details, since, for all the communicants knew, a special and necessary efficacy might reside in the very materials employed.

In this case, however, although millstones came into quite general use, mortars were by no means wholly

discarded. As late as the writing of the Book of Proverbs they were very common contrivances for grinding
corn and their use was apparently not confined to the
poorer classes. Perhaps they were particularly useful
for grains less troublesome than wheat, such as barley
or millet or spelt. But there is nothing to show that
as fine a flour could not be obtained by mortar and
pestle as by two millstones. The manna of the desert,
we are expressly told, could be prepared in either way.
It was evidently a matter of personal choice at all
times whether one contrivance or the other should
be used.

Grinding was women's work, particularly that of
female slaves. In large households there were some
maid-servants who did little else all day. When the
Second Isaiah threatens Babylon with imminent destruction he pictures her as stripped of her finery and
reduced to this most menial of tasks. "Take the millstones and grind meal." But as a mark of humiliation,
young men might be set to perform this service, especially as it was considered particularly hard.

This close association of women with the mill is
illustrated in the story of Abimelech, whom the woman
of Thebez slew by hurling a millstone upon his head,
a story famous in Israel thereafter. She took the
weapon nearest to her hand.

Between coarse meal and fine meal the difference
lay probably in the amount of the grinding. As we
might suppose, the finer flour was for the more delicate

palates of the great or for the religious ritual. As for the process of turning this flour into bread, that is something with which despite our specialization we have not lost all acquaintance. The obvious steps of mixing the flour with water, of kneading it, of setting it to rise, and of baking it we have all observed, although most of us could perform the tasks with only indifferent success.

The reason for using only unleavened bread, as at the ancient Passover festival and generally in ritual observances, is the same as that already mentioned in connection with flint knives and mortars. Unleavened bread is the older kind. But except for ritual purposes, bread was quite generally leavened. It seems that the leaven was merely a piece of the soured dough left from the previous baking. Unless, however, we are prepared to follow the process backward to infinity, somewhere, on some occasion, a loaf must have been leavened for the first time. In that case it seems to have been left to ferment naturally.

This does not sound very palatable and what we read of the process of baking does not increase our desire to change our bread-making for the ancient method. The most primitive fashion was simply to put the kneaded dough on hot ashes and turn it from one side to the other. A little more advanced method was that of baking the loaves in a pan over glowing embers. But side by side with these ways of baking there were also stoves, although they bore an extremely slight resemblance to modern stoves. They seem to have been earthenware jars in the bottom of which hot charcoal had been placed. The loaf might be outside or inside the jar. This sounds like a poor excuse for an oven, but it seems to have sufficed for the preparation of some rather elaborate dishes.

Women, we may assume, did most of the baking, but the art was not so distinctly a woman's business. It was generally assumed that men were reasonably familiar with it. Otherwise the frequent directions found in the Prophets and in the Pentateuch for baking certain cakes must have been a little embarrassing to the men to whom the directions were given. Bakers as a craft were nearly all men, although the royal bakers, perhaps the pastry-cooks, seem to have been women. As a craft we shall have occasion to speak of them later on.

The individual household thus controlled each process from the planting of the seed to the final preparation of bread. The same thing may be said of every other form of food. The pressing of oil from the olive, the treading of the grapes and the making of wine, all were done at home by the service of slaves or members of the family. Similarly, animal food was obtained from cattle which belonged to the household. Here, however, some outside direction was likely to be sought. The slaughter of animals was often a sacrifice, particularly before the time of King Josiah of Judah, when apparently the ritual of sacrifice might be performed anywhere and was not confined to the great altar of the Temple. In such case the selection of the proper sort of animal and perhaps the ritual of the killing itself, could scarcely be accomplished without the supervision of priest or Levite. But except for this religious supervision, the men of the household needed no outside assistance in providing themselves with meat any more than with vegetable food. Slaughtering, dressing and preserving meats were domestic arts.

While animals were slaughtered principally for sacrifice, we cannot suppose that there was no other occasion on which meat was eaten. What became of the less perfect animals, since only those unblemished externally and internally could be sacrificed? Doubtless the rules of *Shehitah* had not attained their present form. And when only one altar existed—the one at Jerusalem—surely all those did not abstain from animal food who had no means of getting to that altar. We must remember, to be sure, that vegetable food was the rule and meat the exception, an exception reserved for feasts, for hospitality to strangers and for religious rites. Yet exceptional or not, it was a well-known form of food and the point for us is the fact that the household was capable of providing it completely and of managing every stage of its preparation.

Domestic control of the food supply in all its stages is outside our experience, but so many of the stages are still matters within our personal observation that we can imagine the others without difficulty. When we contemplate the other great human need, that of clothing, our power to visualize its production fails somewhat. Spinning wheels are now parlor ornaments rather than household utensils. But even spinning demands considerable preliminary steps, most of which have long been withdrawn from the consumer's knowledge. If we take wool as an example we learn that the fleece had to be clipped from the sheep's back, then sorted and classed, washed and carefully dried. It had to be carded, that is, separated into single fibres and these fibres combed into straight yarn. It is this combed yarn that the spindle can unite into long threads.

But we are far from through. The threads must be woven, a process found in essence throughout the world and consisting in making one series of threads cross another at right angles and pushing the two series together so closely that the eye can see no apertures between them at all. Now we have only to tie the ends in order to have a piece of cloth, and if we remember what has been said of biblical garments we see that the shaping and sewing of this cloth into clothing was a relatively simple process. All this sounds technical and a little complicated. But the various steps here specified are the merest outlines of the complicated processes in which today hundreds of thousands of men are engaged. Tremendous machines do what shears and spindle and hand loom once did and an untrained person cannot even follow all the details, much less manage them.

What classes of specially skilled craftsmen do for us now each biblical family did for itself. A certain differentiation took place. Shearing, washing, carding were the work of men; spinning and weaving, of women. Weaving is occasionally spoken of as a masculine task and when weavers were a caste they were all men. But in general a differentiation of this kind maintained itself.

The woolen cloth served other domestic purposes besides those of clothing. There were coverings and hangings, carpets and draperies to be made from it. Sometimes these things need even finer qualities and greater skill than the making of garments. The East still maintains a domestic manufacture of woolen carpets that has been organized into a huge commerce, the making of rugs. Something of the skill and experience now directed by large merchants into international channels was then concentrated on home needs. So far as quality is concerned wool might be delicate lamb's wool or goat or camel's hair. The resultant cloth might then be fine or coarse, but at its finest it was inferior in price to fine linen, the garment of luxury above all others. Even the "silk" which is once mentioned together with it is likely to have been only a particularly delicate variety of linen.

In the case of this linen, the inference we ordinarily draw from ritual uses of an article is contradicted by other facts. When the priests and Levites enter in at the gates of the inner court of the Temple, "they shall be clothed with linen garments. No wool shall come upon them while they minister in the gates." We should be tempted to say that linen is the older vestment if in this same book linen were not mentioned as the dress of especial elegance, and if the cloth of goat's or sheep's wool were not much more likely to have been the dress of the nomads in their pre-Palestinian days. The difficulty can be explained in a number of ways. A possible explanation is that the Canaanite priests got their linen vestments through imitation of Egyptian customs and that in this external matter the Jewish priests followed a prevalent fashion.

Now linen clothing and linen materials were home spun, but not always home grown. Certainly some of the flax came from Egypt through the merchants, but only some of it. After all, flax was not only extensively grown in Palestine and Syria, but there are suggestions that Egypt owed this ancient plant to these Asiatic neighbors. Many households therefore cultivated their own flax as they cultivated their own grain and the sowing and tending of this plant cannot have been very different from any other.

But getting threads out of the stalk of a plant is a much more difficult process than spinning a number of hairs together. It is not given to all of us to follow the details of the mysterious transaction. We read in technical manuals of drying, of "retting", of "scutching"—fearsome words in their sound and appearance. We can only be sure that whatever it is that these words indicate, it was done at home. It was under stalks of flax that, as we recall, Rahab hid the spies on the roof of her house on the wall. And these stalks perhaps appeared finally in the very cloth she hung out dyed in vermilion to indicate that house in Jericho which was to be spared.

That dying and embroidering were home industries goes without saying. Both later became specialized crafts. Embroidery has remained to this day a female and a domestic accomplishment as it was in the main in Israel, in spite of the fact that Oholiab, the son of Ahisamach, first taught it.

The household on its own plot of ground and from it got food and clothing. Could it also provide for an equally fundamental want, that of shelter? Could the *ba'al ha-bayit* make his own house and furniture? Here if anywhere expert hands are needed. It may be that the brick and plaster houses of the poor demanded no great skill, but the poorest of them seem to have been more elaborate than log cabins. In any case, it is certainly taken for granted that the master of the house is also its builder. It is true he may have "built" the house as Solomon "built" the Temple, that is, his part may have consisted in giving orders for its construction. But we may be sure that in many instances the master's actual participation in the physical labor of hewing and hammering was considerable, and that the house was "his" in a sense which will satisfy many social philosophers.

Our picture of the self-sufficient biblical household has, however, been somewhat overdrawn. The specialization and mutual dependence of groups which marks modern society had already begun in biblical times. We may recall the great cities with their royal residences and temple precincts. Hundreds of households, perhaps thousands, were gathered in these quarters. Of one thing we may be sure. Except the slaves, most of this gentry neither toiled nor span. That was at least equally true for those miniature royal residences, the houses of the nobles.

The king had domains of his own from which the needs of his immediate household could have been supplied; but his household was so very large that what one person could do in the ordinary family a whole class was required to do for the king. "He will appoint them unto him for captains of thousands and captains of fifties," Samuel warns the people, "and to plow his ground, and to reap his harvest: and he will take your daughters to be perfumers, and to be cooks, and to be bakers." Here there was already a considerable specialization. But it went further. Solomon's merchants bought linen yarn from Egypt instead of having it spun by his slaves from home grown flax. And probably these merchants bought many other things rather than litter the royal city with the appliances of handicraft.

Not only the king, who by tax and impost amassed

considerable treasure, but any one else in the possession of money or exchangeable commodities would be
tempted to buy goods rather than make them. But in
that case the cities must have contained men who
manufactured and sold and who could scarcely have
done this in addition to the management of such household duties as have been described in this chapter. It
is true that some surplus articles existed everywhere
and these might be disposed of to traders, but casual
production like this could not have been of much economic utility. A highly specialized and numerous class
forming almost a separate community needed groups
of manufacturers and merchants to supply their needs.
The condition of the Temple precincts was such that
it could not have been possible to do enough shearing,
spinning, weaving or planting upon them. The rapidly
increasing number of priests must have soon become
dependent on others for their clothing, their utensils
and a large part of their food, though some of it may
have come to them in kind when tithes became an
established and enforceable imposition.

Then again the wealthy nobles whose houses made
up no small part of the city increased the demand for
specialized occupations. They too had domains outside the city from which they could have supplied their
wants if they were so minded. Some of them undoubtedly did so and the approved conduct of a wealthy man
was to live in patriarchal amplitude like Abraham or
Job. But after all the general use of wealth was then

what it is now, a means for acquiring more wealth. The creation of large estates would generally mean the increase of pasture and pleasure grounds, and the accumulation of silver and gold, which we are told went on apace, would have been futile unless large stocks of purchasable commodities existed.

But such stocks meant production on a scale too great to be satisfied out of self-sufficient households. They imply organized effort and the existence of specialized groups of craftsmen. We hear of many such—carpenters, stone-cutters, builders, wall-builders, plasterers, potters, tanners, fullers, weavers, dyers, perfumers, barbers, bakers and cooks. And these workmen were quite apart from the foreign merchants who dispensed imported wares in competition with the commodities made by some of these craftsmen.

That the craftsmen were associated in something like guilds is highly likely. They lived in separate quarters. The bakers had a street of their own, often enough mentioned in the story of Jeremiah. The fullers used a special field when they washed their wool, a field that went by their name. Only we must not suppose that these groups had anything like the rigid organization of the mediaeval guilds or the modern trade unions. They were not even as definite corporations as those many societies which began to spread throughout the Greek world from the fifth century B. C. E. onward, and into which the Jews of the Dispersion readily entered.

What was the ordinary attitude toward these crafts? Generally in the ancient world manual labor, unless it was agriculture, was semi-servile and correspondingly disesteemed. But there is no direct expression of this disesteem in the Bible. Ben Sira, writing in 200 B. C. E., has as we shall see no high opinion of the mercantile classes, but he shows a marked appreciation of the importance of skilled workers. "Without them," he says, "the city cannot be inhabited," and on another occasion he bids his readers "hate not appointed source of laborious work." What Ben Sira felt on this subject was doubtless shared by the wealthy and educated class to which he belonged. They were tolerant, but Ben Sira's admonition itself implies that gentlemen of his time were inclined to be contemptuous of the labor which ensured their own complete leisure.

One craft was not mentioned in the list just given because it was always something quite special. That was the craft of smiths, of the workers in metal. Theirs, it may well be, was the oldest of all specialized callings. To take iron out of the earth and melt brass out of the stone was a mysterious thing, and to weld this iron and brass into swords and plowshares, vessels and chariots, equally mysterious. The founding of this craft was assigned to the remotest antiquity, to Tubal-Cain, the son of Lamech and the brother of Jubal, so that metal working is made out to be as old as tents and cattle herding, the primitive form of social life. This one art never was a part of the domestic economy and to this extent even the most primitive household was not self-supporting. Not only under Philistine domination, but quite generally, men had to seek the smith to make their swords and utensils, "to sharpen every man his share and his coulter and his ax and his mattock."

In Europe smiths were considered somewhat uncanny. Thousands of legends and superstitions are associated with them. There seems no trace of such feeling in biblical life. The smiths were one class among many, one of the most skilled of the classes, and were regarded as ranking distinctly above the generality of laborers. Nebuchadnezzar deported "the princes and the mighty men of valour and all the draftsmen and the smiths: none remained save the poorest sort of people of the land." In this enumeration smiths are set against all other types of skilled workers taken together, though the word used in the Hebrew text is of very general meaning and may refer to artificers in stone and wood as well. However, the smith was the artificer *par excellence.* Just as in English itself a general word meaning "skilful workman" came to suggest preëminently a worker in metal.

The craftsmen and smiths deported by Nebuchadnezzar were Jews and in the older stories Moses found in Bezaleel the son of Uri skill enough "to work in gold and in silver and in brass and in cutting of stones and in carving of timber." But when Solomon prepared to build the great Temple and his own house, he sent to his royal ally of Tyre with the words: "Thou knowest that there is not among us any that hath skill to hew timber like unto the Zidonians." Half Tyrian too was the Hiram who made the brass work for Solomon. In the further construction many Tyrian builders worked side by side with Solomon's own men. Except for this notable case, the references to craftsmanship imply that its possessors were native and not foreign artificers. Yet the fact that outside help was sought for the two finest structures in Jerusalem is itself significant. Artistic work of the highest grade was most probably foreign. At any rate foreign goods would be prized for their very expensiveness, as they still are all over the world. The limitations which Jewish institutions placed upon artistic development have already been indicated. Jewish craftsmanship might follow foreign models to a certain point but not beyond.

Foreigners came into the land for other purposes than to hew timber and melt brass for the king. The chief of these purposes was trade. And this brings us to an extraordinary characteristic of biblical society, the practical absence of a native merchant class. The Valorous Woman "maketh fine linen and selleth it and delivereth girdles unto the merchant." Who was this merchant? The very word used in both Hebrew and Greek tells us plainly enough. He was a Canaanite, one of the non-Jewish inhabitants of the country, who trod the alleys of every city and performed a function which the disappearing class of peddlers and hucksters performs today. Besides him, there were merchants on a much grander scale, those whose booths lined the market places and who had quarters of their own at all the important gates. They likewise were foreigners, Edomites, Midianites, Syrians of Damascus, Egyptians and Asiatic Greeks. Above all they came from the city "whose merchants were princes, whose traffickers were the honourable of the earth," the magnificent city of Tyre. Tyre itself was the great mart to which surrounding nations streamed, the Israelites along with the others.

But among the Israelites themselves a merchant class developed slowly, and did not appear until very late. Even in pre-Exilic days men must have had things to sell, or they would not have gone to Tyre to dispose of them. But those who went to Tyre exchanged rather than sold and what they bought at home or abroad they bought to consume, not to resell. It was not until the Return that we hear of a definite group within the community called merchants. When the wall is built by Nehemiah, "Between the upper chamber of the corner and the sheep gate, repaired the goldsmiths and the merchants." This was not a large part of the total task and indicates no extensive or powerful corporation. But the members are indubitably Jews and are very different from the foreign merchants whom Nehemiah mentions with vehement disapproval.

Nehemiah disapproved of the Tyrian merchants because they desecrated the Sabbath and tempted Jews to do likewise. But if he had not had this specific grievance against them, he would probably have shared in the prejudice which the craft seems always to have excited in ancient times. In Egypt merchants were also largely foreigners, and resident foreigners were never popular. But in Palestine "the stranger within the gates" was not disesteemed because of alienage. A merchant was looked on askance because his business was in itself not altogether reputable. His temptations were many and his proclivity to yield to them was assumed to be great. Ben Sira was markedly contemptuous and distrustful of the entire class. "A merchant," he says, "shall hardly keep himself from wrong-doing." In saying this he voiced a sentiment common not only to his own time and people but fairly persistent in all societies economically organized in the way biblical society was.

Of a financial class, that is, of professional traders in money, there is no evidence. Rich men, despite the specific prohibitions of the law, lent money and other commodities upon usury, and were bitterly upbraided by prophets and moralists. But they were not bankers. As among the Romans, so to the Jews, banking was a Greek innovation and was probably confined to the Greeks who filled the Levant after the time of Alexander.

The daily occupations of the people, therefore, varied enormously, even if we leave the royal household, and the priesthood, out of account. On the whole, trades and professions made up a very reputable total. But in one vital matter the situation was quite different from our own. Occupations were not fluid. Careers were not selected by free choice. Boys did not speculate on what they would do when they grew up. They were pretty well assured that they would do what they saw their fathers doing, and they would have been startled and alarmed if it had been suggested to them that they might follow a different vocation. The only alternative to their own almost hereditary calling was the dreaded possibility of losing completely their property or position. This involved sinking into mendicancy or the semi-slavery of clientage.

The prospect therefore that presented itself to the dreaming youth of biblical times was rigid enough, even if it generally seemed desirable to him. Was there room for the spirit of adventure? That there were no persons in biblical times to whom the secure routine of a peaceful enjoyment of land was distasteful because of its very security and certainty, is incredible. In the biblical people there were fused the stocks that had from hoary antiquity possessed the land, and the nomad Covenanters of the desert. This latter strain was always present and powerful. Touch with the desert men was never completely lost and was readily enough resumed. Under his vine and fig tree, did no one remember with keen zest the eager and precarious life which preceded the taking of the good land, and which crowded songs and legends with deeds of wild daring and changing color?

Well, for one thing the charm of mere uncertainty was never denied to the man of the Bible. Except at rare intervals, wars and rumors of wars filled the country as they filled all ancient countries. The morrow might bring forth a Scythian, a Syrian, an Egyptian, a Babylonian army to the gates of the city, and as far as those men were concerned who had nothing to do with royal intrigues and dreams of empire, every invasion took them by surprise. This was true of Palestine more than of other lands, and in Palestine more than elsewhere the fervent and constant supplication to God was for "Peace!" and the daily greeting of *Shalom!* was not the announcement of a truce, but a prayer.

Yet peace had dangers that were acutely realized. Suppose wars were to cease, as the prophet sang, and each man were to sit unafraid under his own vine and fig tree. Would there not soon be too many otiose patriarchs, too few fig trees? The latter are after all limited in number. Thousands of years before modern economists attacked the problem, the outstripping of goods by population in any one place was a serious and apparent danger. Artificial means to meet that danger were used throughout the Mediterranean world. Some children were not reared at all. Every now and then a certain number of the inhabitants of a region would be sent out of the city to seek their fortunes elsewhere. The Romans called this custom "a sacred spring" and we may find in it the origin of colonization. Where it was not undertaken in the systematic way so often described in Greek and Roman writings, we know it was frequently resorted to by individual families who sought better homes elsewhere than in the land of their kinsmen. Indeed what else had brought Abraham from Padan-Aram, and what else brought to Canaan the many strangers who dwelt as sojourners and clients?

Of such emigrations forced by economic pressure we hear nothing in the time before the Exile. Periods of prosperity and peace there had indeed been but in spite of the fact that the Israelites reared all their children, ther had been no such overpopulation that the strenuous measures used in ancient cities had to be resorted to. The land still contained empty spaces. Natural causes, the difficulties of ordinary living, famine, war, plagues and pestilence, even when they occurred spasmodically, kept numbers well within excess.

After the Exile, in Judea, a very limited and difficult soil soon pressed the population hard. In spite of local disputes the Persian over-lordship kept peace, and once the little state got on its feet, it increased rapidly. The early Greek period—which is at the very end of our survey—knew of emigrations on a large scale, half voluntary and half forced, to the many new foundations of the Greek and Macedonian kings in Egypt and Syria. And that process had begun before among individuals, chiefly in the case of soldiers. For there was always that outlet for spirits to whom the routine of a successful life was inadequate. Men who could fight, *anshe hayil*, were in demand everywhere. We find a Jewish military colony at the first cataract of the Nile almost before the Exile, and we have every reason to believe that there were others. The soldier emigrants who sought service and the chance of fame and fortune in foreign lands were numerous even when conditions at home were prosperous, since prosperity meant larger families and since goods increased in a smaller ratio than population.

We may say therefore that if occupations seemed fixed by hereditary position and the ideal of society seemed somewhat uniform, there was one real career open to the talents. Adventure and possible wealth and power lay abroad, at the risk of one's life, it is true, but life was not so greedily clung to then as in our days. And for this career of the soldier even Ben Sira has no condemnation. Apparently it seemed to him like the manual trades, a necessary task which some must take up, and which those had best engage in who were unfitted for other things.

To be wealthy even in ancient times meant to be relieved from the need of daily labor. But a real leisure class, such as that to which Ben Sira himself belonged, did not develop until after the Exile. Ben Sira despised merchants, looked down on laborers with benignant tolerance and faintly approved of soldiers. One may ask, what did he do himself? His answer would have been simple. He sought Wisdom. He was a *hakam*.

Of this study of Wisdom we have had occasion to speak before. One thing about it cannot be said too soon. It was not a career. The double purpose that the *hakam* had, that of seeking wisdom for himself and of imparting it to others, was never to be a means of securing a livelihood. In the Greek world of the fifth century the Greek *sophistes* was in name and function almost exactly parallel to the *hakam*. But the sophist succeeded despite difficulties and objections in making his expertness in wisdom the basis of a profitable profession, and in this he was followed with a certain indirection by those who changed the title of "sophist" into that of "philosopher." This the *hakam* never succeeded in doing, even when his honorary prefix of *Rabbi* became the name of a profession. In this case as in others Hellenism proved more practically minded than Hebraism.

The profession of Wisdom, too, contained within itself another profession, which has in modern times lost something of its ancient dignity. This was the profession of the law. When all law, no matter how concrete and technical, was the law of God, the *hakam* was concerned with contracts and damages as much as with the nature and goal of life. Perhaps as early as talmudic times a group of men had already disengaged themselves to whom law was more interesting than ethics or theology. In biblical times, Wisdom was undifferentiated.

The other great liberal profession of modern times, that of physicians, had to detach itself from less respectable associations. In the state with which biblical people were most associated, the great land of Egypt, physicians were astoundingly numerous and astoundingly specialized. There was a different physician for every part of the body. But it is likely that these "physicians" were in part at least magicians and embalmers—that is, connected in some way with the priestly cult. In Israel, too, priests apparently practised an art that was partly the application of prayer and charms and partly the use of a very ancient herb medicine. And the "physicians" whom King Asa ought not to have consulted in his extremity were likewise in all probability magicians as much as masters of medicine. But that skilled and experienced men existed who used therapeutic arts as well as a real surgery is implied in a number of biblical references.

It is curious to note that a tendency arose among excessively pious people in the times after the Exile to regard the aid of physicians as a sinful attempt to interfere with the plans of Providence. Ben Sira, who was as pious as one could wish, in a sober and sensible fashion, took pains to defend physicians. "Acquaint thyself with a physician," he says, "before thou have need of him, for him also hath God ordained. For from

God, the healer is made wise. . . . The Lord created medicines out of the earth and let not a prudent man despise them." The Talmud also emphatically announces that the art of the physician is sanctioned by the Torah.

But we must not think of physicians at any time as scientifically trained men forming an honorable and dignified profession, access to which was open to all who desired it. It was apparently a craft, a little less menial than the manual arts, free from the imputations of trickery made against merchants, but something less than a calling befitting a gentleman.

A little of the traffic in formulas and amulets clung to it for many centuries. Indeed, even among the Greeks, in spite of the remarkable beginnings made by Hippocrates, a contemporary of Ezra, medicine suffered a scientific relapse which lasted until well after biblical times. It may be said that physicians were not as a class highly regarded or deserving of much confidence anywhere in the Eastern Mediterranean, except in Egypt.

In actual numbers of different occupations the society of Bible times was not so radically different from our own as we might have supposed. But its attitude was quite different. It had no sense of modern interdependence. The prospects of life were less speculative. Precarious in a measure life certainly was, but its precariousness was due to external and incalculable events. Business panics, industrial depressions had no existence. And above all the vast majority lived in an obvious and conscious association with the land on the face of which they labored and from the fat of which they drew their sustenance.

CHAPTER X

HOUSE AND HOME

IN the country, house and workshop were the same. Such buildings or tents as existed were devised primarily for the work of the fields, to shelter the men in inclement weather, to protect the herds, to store the food, to press the grapes. And they rarely went beyond the limit just necessary to fulfil these essential purposes.

In the city men who had actual occupations likewise carried them on at home as far as it was feasible. But the city was not really intended for men with daily occupations. We shall have to concern ourselves principally in this chapter and in the following one with the minority rather than with the great mass of the people, with those whom we might call men of leisure, but whose lives furnish many points of comparison with our own.

The master of the house spent his morning in the market attending public business or hearing the news of the day. He returned at noon to a meal likely enough to be frugal unless he was bringing guests with him—and that he was not likely to do. After the meal he took his siesta in some retired alcove or in an upper room if the house was grand enough to have one. Such house business as the direction of the labors of his family, the examination of accounts, must have come later as well as that teaching of his children which became so urgent and holy a duty. We can scarcely doubt that many men took all these tasks lightly and that the hours after the siesta became insensibly a time for idle amusements and not for the fulfilling of onerous obligations. But in any case this was the time of the day in which, unless specific business called him elsewhere, the master of the house was at home.

The cool of the evening found him in the court of his house or on the roof in his family circle. It was one of the pleasantest hours of the day and was often passed in mere physical enjoyment of the air's grateful freshness. The *hakam*, if he had visitors who were to be guests at supper, used this time and place for much of the profitable discourse which cultured gentlemen enjoyed. And those whose chief concern was not wisdom occupied the agreeable period according to their lights, which often led them, we may suspect, to no occupation at all.

Since we have followed a substantial citizen into his house we might look about us at the house itself. Our initial caution about confusing terms is more necessary here than elsewhere. For nothing really less like our idea of a house could well be imagined than that which was so called in the Bible. The point was that the very function the building subserved was really quite different. In those days men did not construct houses in the conscious expectation of spending a large part of their daily lives in them. The part of their lives which interested them most was to be spent in the open, not under a roof. A house was a place of retirement.

Houses in the country were often mere huts and seem to have been largely built on the model of the tents they replaced. But the city house did not develop from the tent. The basic structure of the city house may be said to be a walled court, into which a number of roofed alcoves or apartments opened. These apartments were always small, sometimes quite tiny. They were meant to fit precisely the specific purpose for which they were made, whatever the purpose was. Generally they were open on the side toward the court. Light and air entered from that quarter and not from the outside.

The result was that the outer walls of the house were bleak and forbidding. This, we may remember, was intentional. It was no part of any man's purpose to invite attention to the place of his retirement. What we should call the door—in most cases the only door —of the house, was a gateway leading into a narrow passage. Frequently it was oblique, so that the events of the house proper, or the court which was the house's heart, would not be open to the inspection of casual passers-by. Of these, incidentally, there would in the nature of things be very few. Any one found skulking along the narrow lanes that separated most houses would readily be credited with a sinister purpose, and in many cases quite justly. The burglar of ancient times was not a man who broke into a house but one who dug an entry under the wall. The building material was clay bricks or limestone for the poor, and hewn stone for the wealthy. Wood was freely used for panels, for ceilings, for columns and for ornaments, but not for the framework itself.

All this would apply to almost the entire Mediterranean region as well as to Palestine. The great difference between a Greek or an Egyptian house and a Jewish one lay in the ornamentation. There could be no statuary among the Jews, and the sort of carving in relief which was permitted, a carving which completely excluded animal figures, was likely to be monotonous. Whatever designs were used were painted in bright colors, whether they were animal forms used in defiance of law or any other kind. Indeed even if the inner walls were not carved at all, they would be painted, perhaps simply tinted. Vermilion seems to have been the favorite color for this purpose.

There is much reason to believe that individuals varied in the strictness with which they observed the second commandment. Except in cases of downright idolaters, free-standing statues were probably never found. But many who deemed themselves worshippers of the Lord probably permitted themselves considerable latitude in painting and in carving in relief. The prophetic attitude on that point was undoubtedly one of stern reprobation, but it was long before this view became universally dominant.

Still the actual amount of ornamentation in a Jewish house was relatively small and its artistic character must have been notably below the standard of Egypt or of Greece. The sheen of polished woods in the ceilings, in the doorposts, in the floors, probably sufficed for elegance and beauty to the minds of most men, even the wealthy. Color and decoration would more naturally be found in the hangings and carpets that covered floor and walls.

Just as the shell of the house was designed for a practical purpose, so its furniture seemed little calculated to gather about it the sentimental associations of that of our houses. The nomad Covenanters sat on mats on the bare ground and the peasants continued the custom. The city dweller certainly did not. He sat on benches or even chairs and these chairs might become thrones for special occasions; and when fashions changed, and he reclined on couches, these couches, like the chairs, were decorated with embroidered coverlets and made comfortable with pillows. Upon such a couch he might sleep at night unless he was a rather grand personage and had a separate bedroom. Grand personages, however, were very likely to ape foreign fashions and the houses of such men tended to become like Mesopotamian, Egyptian and finally like Greek houses.

Couches were sometimes built against the wall, whether they were couches used solely for meals or for both meals and sleep. In the main, however, beds were movable, like the bed on which Saul wished David to be brought to him. When Elisha was entertained at Shunem by a great lady there, in the little chamber that was built for him she placed a bed and a table and a stool and a candlestick. But even splendid beds were used as divans on occasions. To Amos the height of luxury was illustrated by those men "who sit in Samaria in the corner of a couch or on the silken cushions of a bed." As we rise in the scale of sumptuousness the couches may be of ivory or of silver and gold, in which case we must suppose slabs of these materials laid on a wooden framework. They were often covered "with tapestry and carved work, with fine linen of Egypt."

Thus couches formed the most costly and the most prominent part of the house furniture. But as we have seen from the chamber of Elisha, they were not the only articles. Tables are frequently mentioned and nearly always in connection with meals, except where the tables of the shew-bread are meant. If the singular is used literally, tables varied enormously in size, from the table of Jezebel at which four hundred men were entertained, or Nehemiah's, which feasted more than one hundred and fifty, to Elisha's little table in his upper room. But of course, the word may be used in a very general way or else the tables may have been merely planks laid upon temporary supports. We may guess that generally the tables formed no part of the visible furniture of the house but were brought in for each meal or perhaps for each course. They certainly were low, as though they had originally been intended for people who sat on the floor, and they needed little increase of height when the diners sat or reclined, because they were even then rather serving tables than dining tables.

Elisha's little room, we recall, needed only a "candle-stick and a chair, bed and table" to be completely furnished, even by one who wished to do the prophet honor. The word used here is *menorah*, a word otherwise confined to the famous candelabrum of the Temple. But neither this word nor the others similarly translated mean candlestick at all. They are in every case lamps, although doubtless rude and primitive enough. They consisted of a little clay bowl with sides curving upward in which a wick of flax was placed. The lamps were filled with olive oil and kept burning all night. Perhaps the word *menorah* was used for the great lamp in the sanctuary and for this lamp of Elisha because in both cases the lamp was supported on some sort of a stand, while the ordinary lamp stood free. There were also torches made of pine or rushes. These must have been saturated with pitch or oil at the end, else they could scarcely have served the purpose of lighting at all without risk to the holder. Evidently they were an inferior and cheaper form of illumination.

If we add the chests or coffers in which clothing or other valuable things were kept, we have practically exhausted the household furniture. That these chests were themselves carved or painted is suggested in one biblical passage, but the text is doubtful and it may be that the words refer to the contents of the coffer rather than to its exterior.

The absence of stoves for purposes of heating need not surprise us. Mediterranean countries have, even in this age of technical development, only imperfectly solved the problem of keeping houses warm in cold weather. In ancient and biblical days there was no serious attempt to do so. In the north and in the hills, cold was not infrequent in the rainy season, but there was no other means of warming a house than by bringing braziers of live coals into a room. That can have served only a brief emergency. In general people were compelled to keep warm by wrapping themselves in mantles just as they might do outside the house.

In this house of open courts and alcove chambers there were also inner rooms and upper rooms. A large house might have several rooms which were entered through others and which could therefore be completely shut off from the rest of the building. Into such a room the young prophet brought Jehu when he anointed him King, and in a similar chamber Ben-Hadad hid at Aphek after his crushing defeat. Rooms like these were few and exceptional. The purpose of the house was privacy but privacy for the entire household. It was only rarely that the individual found it necessary to withdraw from the other members of his family into such an enclosed and secret place as an inner room.

The upper rooms served a somewhat different purpose. The little chamber made for Elisha was an upper room. David ascended to one in order to weep for Absalom. But although in these cases retirement was what was desired, the upper chambers were made as much for their coolness and their access to the roof as for their secrecy. We must remember that usually upper chambers did not form a continuous upper story, but were special erections on a part of the house and often merely furnished shade to those who were using the roof. They were an especial mark of wealth and luxury. They are pointedly mentioned by Jeremiah as the ostentation of men who build their house by unrighteousness and their upper rooms by wrong.

So we can follow Ehud when he entered the upper chamber of King Eglon. He evidently first came into the court in which he received permission to have his private audience. Access to the upper chamber where the king happened to be could be gained only through the porch or balcony which projected into the court. By stairs or ladder Ehud ascended to this porch and opened the door of the room, which he carefully locked behind him. He left by exactly the same way that he came, and he needed no means of escaping directly to the street, since the king's death was not known for hours after. While this incident is ascribed to an early period, the house in which it took place is of the type assumed to be generally familiar. All upper rooms, we must suppose, were constructed in this fashion.

Could the word "home" be applied to a house so built and so used? Could men form sentimental attachments, as they so often do now, to the actual structure of these buildings, to their walls and rafters? The ancient passionate devotion to the city in its physical aspect is well-known, but it was a devotion to the site itself, like the love a man might have for an ancestral field on which his fathers had labored, like the love of Naboth for the vineyard he would not surrender to the king. But that is something less than the attachment to one's house which is so common among modern social emotions. A fine house was a matter of pride and if built under proper auspices, a good and meritorious work in the eyes of the Lord, although we suspect that the Lord has here succeeded to the position of the ancient *Baalim* of the land. Such merit as one might earn by the erection of a house was the right of the actual builder. Deuteronomy provides that, if a soldier had built a new house and had not dedicated it, he "go and return to his house lest he die in the battle and another man dedicate it."

Equally the ancient belief in the responsibility of inanimate things still clung to the people and was applied particularly to a house. A house would be a house of blood if a fatal accident occurred in it, and would communicate its uncleanness to its inhabitants. A man was therefore bidden to erect battlements for his roof, "that thou bring not blood upon thy house, if any man fall from thence." Similarly the death of

Hiel's two sons by accidents of construction is still the better explanation of the curse laid upon Jericho's rebuilding. The city was tainted with blood as Joshua had foretold it would be.

Of course the out-door experience which filled most of a man's life was reason enough to explain the relative lack of sentimental attachment to the house. It must have been different for a woman, of whom the highest praise was that "her feet abide in the house." And staying there, she could scarcely do otherwise than entwine some of her affections about it. The situation was the same in the neighboring regions of the world. We know the tragic story of Troy in Vergil's version of it, how the doomed city sinks in fire, how the Greeks burst into Priam's palace and how when the doom is certain, "the terrified women dart in all directions throughout the vast palace, seize the pillars in a close embrace and print kisses upon them." That was quite in the ancient manner—for women, and would have seemed excessive for men. We may be sure that many a Jewish woman found in the homely familiarity of her utensils and her house, the bare rude walls, the coarse woolen coverings, the same outlet for her tenderness as her sisters did in Greek lands, and indeed as they do in more familiar places and more modern days.

CHAPTER XI

MEALS

RUDE and uncivilized men eat when and as they can, often alternating between periods of stoically borne famine and ravenous surfeit. But settled life and a fair assurance of subsistence brings routine in the taking of food as in most other things.

Again we must transcend the limits of the little country between the desert and the sea. The entire Eastern Mediterranean knew of two meals, the morning meal and the evening meal. The Greek translators of the Bible called the former *ariston* and the latter *deipnon*, words which we are prone to translate as "dinner" and "supper", although neither word really suggests the character of the meal. The suggestion that we call the *ariston* "breakfast" is however equally bad.

In the first place, we must remember that this system of a morning and an evening meal belongs to the city. In the fields the character of the labor determined the time of eating, and the natural pause during the noon-day heat suggested that break in the day as a convenient dining hour, as well as the obvious break after sundown, when the day's work was over. But plainly a noon-day meal and an evening one implied a light breakfast on rising, and thus we have something that looks very much like our modern system of three daily meals.

But the likeness is deceptive. The breakfast was not a meal at all, but merely a snatch taken casually by the laborer before going out to the fields, without formality and perhaps alone. Again the noon-day meal was simple and frugal as well as unceremonious. The laborers sat down on the earth at the "time of eating" under the shade of a tree, dipped their pieces of bread in a bowl of vinegar, and took the parched corn from the master's hand; after which they went on directly to their tasks. The evening meal seems to have included wine and, for the more well-to-do peasants, meat as well. Among the poorer men it was a slightly richer variant of the noon-day meal, except that it seems always to have involved a certain amount of ceremony, perhaps the "washing of the hands". This custom certainly existed at the end of our biblical period and may have arisen much earlier in spite of the fact that the canonical books of the Bible do not mention it.

It will be noticed that I have spoken of Greek names for these meals but not of Hebrew names. That is because the Bible has no names for them at all, not even a word for "meal" in general. This seems very strange in view of the fact that the two meals mentioned were almost universal and in view of their obvious importance in determining the character of the day. Perhaps the word for "meal" used in the Talmud, *se-*

'*udah*, which properly means "refreshment", is much older than it seems.

When was the morning meal? The hour varied, but it was neither the informal breakfast that a man might take at rising, nor the noon-day meal or luncheon so familiar to us. In later days it was served when the master returned from his morning prayer at the synagogue or from his visit to the market, about ten o'clock in the forenoon. Guests might well be received at it, but it was not the meal to which guests of distinction would ordinarily be invited, unless they had been encountered casually.

The great meal of the day was the evening one, the *deipnon*. For men of means it followed the evening sacrifice and therefore would certainly be a flesh meal, and even when the religious reform of Josiah precluded animal sacrifice except at Jerusalem, it was likely to have meat as one of the courses. Even to Elijah in the wilderness itself the ravens brought the usual evening repast of bread and flesh.

This meal was elaborate enough, whether the occasion was a festive one or not. Of course we must remember that our information is largely derived from the customs of men of wealth and rank. We have seen that the manners of the country contrasted with those of the town in more than one respect, and we should not forget that the "people" proper, that is, the great majority of the people of biblical times, were country dwellers, and poor. However, the customs based upon the usages of the great tend to become general. If we attempt to follow the details of a meal, it will naturally be a meal at a city house and at the house of some dignitary, and one may reasonably suppose that even poor families imitated this model as far as they could.

The master may have spent the hot afternoon in resting and perhaps in conversation with his family, in the instruction of his children, in reading or being read to. Toward sundown he has arisen for the evening sacrifice or prayer. That accomplished, he has retired to prepare himself for the *deipnon*. The real preparations had of course been going on apace without his lordly supervision. Perhaps even in earlier days, the meat course was not of necessity flesh of a newly sacrificed victim, though it was often so. At any rate, the *shulhan'aruk*, "the spread table", showed many other dishes, fish of many varieties, vegetables in every form, fruit, honey, cakes and wine. Slaves and women had been busy, perhaps for hours, in arranging all these things so that the diners might not be delayed.

The guest arrived and was greeted by the master himself with a kiss. He was then ushered into the vestibule where he removed his sandals and washed his feet in the basin the slaves presented to him. His host might himself perform this office if he wished to do him particular honor. Then came the marshalling of precedence and place. Our national informalities make it hard to realize that these things seemed of first rate importance. Yet in European countries it would be easier to understand, and even we have retained a certain ceremony as to the place of honor at the host's right. That was the case also in ancient Israel; the place of distinction was at the host's right hand, and the other guests sat at a distance from the head in inverse proportion to their rank. When the royal palace was the royal tent and life was a continuous skirmish, the host sat with his back to the wall, facing the entrance, and was thus doubly protected from a surprise attack. The most favored of his guests were therefore equally protected. Later, in the houses of great cities, it is likely that, however the tables were arranged, the host was nearly in the center and the lines of diners ranged from him to the door.

The guests seem to have placed themselves without direction, except in rare instances. It was a matter of etiquette to know where one belonged and a mark of the utmost rudeness to secure a higher place than the proper one. Against this rudeness frequent admonitions are directed by ancient moralists, and since politeness consisted then as now in professing humility toward one's equals, we may imagine a certain amount of deferential bowing and gesturing while the diners seated themselves.

As far as the courses were concerned, it is obvious that a fixed sequence implied a long habit of banquets and a high development of urban life. A great deal of variation was permitted. When one course was completed the slaves cleared the tables and replenished them. In later times when Greek customs were generally followed, the tables were themselves removed and new ones brought in laden with the new courses. And in these same later times the ancient fashion and the present fashion of sitting on chairs at the table made way for the Greek custom of reclining on couches.

This habit of reclining spread rapidly over the whole Mediterranean as a fashion of the highest elegance—why, it is not easy to guess. It seems very uncomfortable to us, even if we supply the couch with cushions and pillows in plenty. What makes it most uncomfortable is our method of using knives and forks. They are certainly not readily managed in a position that is neither upright nor fully supine. The ancient manner, which knew nothing of knife and fork, makes a reclining posture less awkward, though even then it seems scarcely a desirable way and in all likelihood at every interruption in the banquet the diner was fain to relieve somewhat his cramped muscles.

It is, however, not the posture but the absence of table implements that would seem the most extraordinary difference between an ancient meal and our own. The biblical people, from king to slave, ate with their fingers, as we remember mediaeval lords and ladies used to eat, and as Turkish pashas ate until very recently. If they had soup, they dipped their bread into it and so consumed it. Spoons, which existed, seem to have been used for medicine only, just as knives and forks existed only for kitchen use. Dining even in elegant establishments was therefore a rather messy affair, and it has been suggested that the "washing of the hands" which later became so prominent a ritual matter, was originally necessitated by the actual conditions of taking food. Sponges were certainly in use at one time and there was frequent wiping of the hands with napkins.

When we read of ancient life we are likely to find a certain emphasis laid on excesses in eating and drinking. Ancient luxury is most frequently symbolized for us in a banquet and extravagant stories are told of the vast sums squandered by wealthy Greek or Roman debauchees in pampering their appetites. Gluttony became a fine art carried to a literally disgusting perfection. Excesses were of course not unknown even in ancient Israel. The drunkards of Ephraim are not spared by Isaiah or Amos. But the most notable thing about the ancient Jews was that this form of excess did not prevail among them to anything like the extent that it did among their neighbors.

Not that they were averse to the pleasures of the table. Moral teachers commend discrimination and care in the selection of dishes as they deprecate fastidiousness and as they condemn excess. "Be the first to leave off eating," suggests Ben Sira. This was not merely sound sense. It was also good table

manners, on which, as we know, the old gentleman set
great store.   The dietary laws were not as complicated
as those of a later day, but their existence already
provided a certain selection and supervision of the
most important of the viands.   In fact the compara-
tive self-control of even wealthy Jews in this respect
was widely known.   "Their princes ate in due season,
for strength and not for drunkenness."

Among the pleasures of the table that were com-
mendable if partaken of in measure and severely re-
proved if that measure was exceeded, was wine.
Mediterranean people were and still are temperate in
their use of wine.   The Jews seem to have used it
freely at their meals.   Goblets were passed to the
waiting guests before the meal proper began, and wine
mixed with aromatic herbs was an important part of
the concluding courses.   Whether they drank it neat
or mixed with water, as the Greeks did, is open to
question.   The point is that gentlemen did not get
drunk and that those who did were not regarded as
having yielded to an amiable weakness, but as being
stupid or vicious.

The elaborate rules of a Greek symposium with its
master of the feast, its studied etiquette and its op-
portunity for stimulating discourse, were perhaps
never fully taken over by the Jews.   But in the last
century or so of what we may call biblical times, the
institution was adopted, in part at least.   Ben Sira
mentions a master of the feast, and that implies both

the ceremony and the gaiety of the Greek banquet. Garlanded and anointed, their robes and their persons heavily perfumed, the banqueters of whom Ben Sira speaks discussed wisdom, as the guests of Phaedrus in Athens spoke of love or mathematics, except that the former spoke Aramaic or Hebrew and the latter spoke Greek. But the Athenians were following a native custom and the Jerusalemites were with indifferent success imitating a foreign one.

One other pleasure of the table was of more ancient origin, and that was delight in music. Skilful musicians gladdened the heart of King David, as he had himself soothed his royal master by the same means. Guests would hardly be invited to a dinner unless such means of entertainment had been provided. Doubtless in later and luxurious times the entertainment became the chief thing, and dancing girls and more elaborate amusements took the place of the ancient minstrel and his harp. This too was an excess in what was in itself a reasonable pleasure. It lies somewhat outside of our story, since the biblical accounts say nothing of it, but the general repute of the later Jews acquits them of any undue development of this form of entertainment.

The talmudic treatise on "Blessings", *Berakot*, has much to say of ritual at meals. This ritual became more and more elaborate in mediaeval times and observant Jews today devote a very large portion of their meals to numerous graces and special prayers.

It is not likely that these prevailed to anything like such an extent in biblical times, although the talmudic doctors were at great pains to find biblical passages in support of the existing rules. Yet a certain amount of religious ritual was indispensable to every ancient meal and particularly to every ancient meal in Israel. Even the Greeks poured libations when they drank. The Jews uttered prayers and "sanctified" themselves before the meal and when they drank their wine after the meal itself was over. Their God did not—as often among the Greeks—come down to share their banquets, but food and drink in their season were His gift, and only the overweening and the uncultivated forgot to acknowledge it.

CHAPTER XII

FOLKLORE AND SUPERSTITION

I HAVE tried to omit as far as possible any account of the religious beliefs and observances of the people. In the case of any people that must be a serious omission. In the case of the people of biblical times, it is almost an absurd one. No people of antiquity, we generally and correctly suppose, ever worked their religious customs and convictions into their daily lives so thoroughly as did the Jews. Indeed the preoccupation of the Jews with religion was so great that their religious practices and beliefs have become a vast subject, far transcending in importance anything else about them, and filling thousands of books in hundreds of languages.

We may therefore take it for granted. It is the life of the Jews outside of their religious life that we should like to get a glimpse of, and we must endeavor to separate from their activities most of those we should call religious. It is not easy to do. It would not have been easy to do with any ancient people. The men of old did little without the gods or without the consciousness of having as witnesses or participants their superhuman and invisible fellow citizens. And they took it so much as a matter of course that they could scacely have told whether in any given case an act was a religious one or not. And what is true of Greeks and Romans and Egyptians is true in an intensified form of Jews. Yet we must remember that it seems the more so for an accident of transmission. We have only a fragment of the literature of the Jews in the Bible. Strictly speaking, it is an anthology, a selection, and, we may say, it is in part an anthology for a religious purpose. We need scarcely wonder that the account it gives emphasizes the religious element in the life of the people.

Now, that all ancient Jews were religiously minded, I venture to doubt; just as I doubt that all ancient Greeks were artists or all ancient Romans jurists. I suppose it must be true that a larger number were interested in religious matters than among other peoples; but it was almost surely only a minority that took their beliefs very hard and never moved or acted except as religious convictions impelled them. At any rate, they were only a minority in the settled life in Canaan, whatever may have been the case when the fervent Covenanters first swept over the Jordan.

The religious life of the Jews, their Sabbaths and festivals, their pilgrimages to Jerusalem, or to Dan and Bethel, their sacrifices and their abstentions, their prayers and psalms, we shall take for granted and assume to be known. And their religious struggles, the "prophetic" movement, which maintained and established in final triumph the separate character of the Covenant God, enlarging the conception of His

power and character as their own minds were enlarged
by culture and exalted by passionate zeal—all this is
too big a subject for our present investigation. But
we must give a brief glance at the vestiges of other and
older customs which lingered when people already
knew better things and influenced their lives when
they professed that they had abandoned the old beliefs.

It would be sheer hypocrisy to be shocked at the
continued existence of magic and superstition. Modern Europeans living for fifteen centuries and more
under a system that claims to account exhaustively
for all the relations between God and men have retained an unbelievable number of practices both unrecog-
nized and repudiated by their religious convictions.
We shall therefore find it quite natural that the phrase
"Thou shalt have no other God before Me", was not
taken by earnest persons to imply a complete repudiation of charm and spell, of diviner and witch-finder.
As the religious organization progressed, it is true, and
as the prophets grew more and more fervid and
zealous, all supernatural things that were not from
God became first suspect, then abominable; but even
then, men who believed themselves devout allowed
themselves to practise a few ancient customs furtively.

First of all, almost every one believed in dreams,
and for such a belief there was ample warrant in the
sacred Scriptures. We need but think of the dreams
of Jacob, of Joseph, of King Abimelech, of Pharaoh, of
Laban, of Gideon. Dreams were sent by God, we

must suppose, in every case. The difficulty was in understanding them. For that, one had to be "wise" in every sense in which the word can be understood. Men professing to be wise in this sense abounded, but it was a difficult and dangerous profession. In many stories it is the real interpreter whom God inspires who is triumphantly proven right against the helpless wise man, or the deceitful false prophet.

The purpose of the interpretation was to guide conduct. It is not so much that man yearns to know the future, as is often said; but rather that when he begins an undertaking of doubtful issue he would like to be sure of a successful outcome or else abandon it. If he dreams at this time, as he is very likely to do, or if at any time he has a peculiarly vivid or strange dream, he would very much like to know what the dream portends, since he is quite used to the fact that one set of images may be used as symbols for a wholly different set. And no doubt there were many surreptitiously wise men who would tell him the meaning for a consideration.

Against the false interpreters of dreams the prophet inveighs, but against the importance of dreams and the reality of their divine origin no prophetic voice is ever raised. In the course of time, as it became apparent to many prudent persons that "dream interpreters" were rarely right and that when their interpretations were not palpably wrong they were generally meaningless, sensible people ceased to consult them. Those men who might be supposed to have means of divine communication, seers and priests, could not in the nature of things do more than offer help when moved thereto by the Spirit of God. It will be noticed that in the later historical narratives we hear of no successful interpretation of dreams, and that the prophets see waking visions and do not dream dreams. Yet belief in dreams was ineradicable in all men's minds, and in post-biblical times popular legend and story were full of ominous dreams and brilliant interpretations. Indeed such beliefs have never died out and in some of the cruder applications of an ultra-modern psycho-analysis we see the old *hartumim* with all their regalia and a great many of their ancient rules for understanding symbols.

The belief in dreams very easily adapted itself to the new faith of the invading Israelites. Communication with God was a certainty and this means an obvious road of communication. The same could be said for many another form of what we call divination. One took rods or arrows or colored stones and picked some of them out or let them fall at random, with an earnest prayer that if they fell in a specific way it should portend one of several lines of action. Would God refuse to connect the apparently random result with the desired meaning? And when the petitioner was magistrate or priest speaking in behalf of the congregation in a solemn ritual of invocation, the likelihood of divine guidance was practically assured.

Indeed such divination by Urim and Thummim, by ephods or other means, had become a fixed if slightly dubious part of the ritual, and to deny that God could indicate His will in this apparently trivial fashion would have seemed blasphemous.

But whereas dreams never ceased to be considered divine admonitions, the practice of divination by rods and by lots was soon withdrawn by orthodox opinion from any but public officers. It came to be believed that this deliberate request for an answer from God was a flagrant impertinence, except on the part of the anointed or inspired mouthpiece of God. It was not merely wicked but dangerous; for who knew what evil influences might seize the way of communication which God rejected? That such evil influences existed, the great masses certainly believed long before they had learned to call them demons and devils; and these same masses found it easier to think of the heathen gods as real, but ill-willed and harmful beings, than as simple nonentities.

Then too these same heathen gods in their crudest and oldest form, in the form of little images or fetishes, were kept in the houses of the more ignorant and superstitious. It was probably not until King Josiah's time, almost 600 B. C. E., that it was unlawful to have the images called *teraphim*—and the older writers of Genesis and Judges apparently saw nothing wrong in the practice. Some people no doubt worshipped these *teraphim*, but the majority regarded them rather as

bringers of good luck.   King Josiah and his reformers
would have thought them as inoffensive as we now
consider the horse-shoe on a farmer's barn, if it had
not been for the obvious suggestion of worship which
the mere presence of any image presented.

The man in the street knew that there were regular
means of divine communication, by lots, the Urim and
Thummim, which it was not for him, but for the
priests, to attempt; by dreams which came to him
freely but which he could rarely understand; and by
visions of prophets and seers which were forced on him
unbidden by strange and enthusiastic men who stirred
him to violent advocacy or opposition.   But if these
were the regular means there were also irregular ones.
We cannot say whether the wizards, witches, necro-
mancers, snake-charmers, who appear under so many
names in the Bible, asserted that it was the Covenant
God whose will they could determine or whose inter-
position they could almost force by their mutterings
and spells and passes.   They may well have done so.
But in most cases they must have discreetly withheld
the name of what god it was whom they promised to
summon, and confined their pretensions to promises
of tangible rewards.   Most of them were, like those
who used the *teraphim*, quite public in their practice
until the time of Josiah.   After that time they slunk
into corners, but we may be sure did a thriving business in the calamitous days which followed.   For, that
they had a real power—even if it was directed to ill

ends—pious people were not prepared to deny. Had not the Egyptian enchanters, worsted to be sure in the end, matched miracle with miracle against even Moses and Aaron?

There was also a kind of white magic, innocent in itself, which was wide-spread. People wore amulets which kept off harm and sickness, things that could easily be made orthodox by being inscribed with a text or a divine name. They believed certain plants or animals had a particular efficacy. We know of the mandrakes which Rachel ate to insure children, and in an apocryphal book many plants are referred to as healing herbs. This may have been a form of medicine rather than magic and brings us again to that association between physicians and charm-mongers of which we have already spoken.

Lastly, men were much concerned with magic words. Blessings and curses seemed to some to have a kind of blind force in themselves, going out no one knew whither and capable of being deflected, often of being turned back on their origin, thus coming home to roost, as we say of curses. So oaths and vows were half magical, binding in themselves, without regard to the divine power invoked. Jephthah's vow was a wicked one but the readers of his story never asked why God permitted its performance. It bound him indissolubly because it had been uttered.

This is not a very formidable list of superstitions. There is no peasant community of the present day which does not have many hundred times as many. And if we keep in mind modern "cults", spiritualism, occultism, and the like, it is hard to see that educated men in Europe and America have much with which to reproach the Judean peasants of twenty-five centuries ago. It is not likely, to be sure, that our account of biblical magic and folklore is an exhaustive one. Sir James Frazer wrote of the Folklore in the Old Testament in three great volumes. But the folklore which he describes and for which he finds such wide-spread illustrations throughout the known world consists rather of customs which had been worked into the established religion or which, as he infers, lay at the root of certain rites and sacred legends. Thus the covenant of Abraham, the mark of Cain, the boring of a servant's ear, the water of purification, the contest of Jacob, are similar to legends and customs found anywhere from the Pampas to Tahiti. That is, however, rather a question of religious origins, a vast subject, far too vast for us to meddle with in such an account as the present. Again behind a great many of the legends collected by Professor Ginzberg there are obviously superstitions, rites and beliefs like those known in many other regions. These are post-biblical in the form in which they have come down to us and we can only guess to what extent they are survivals from biblical life.

Yet we must recall the qualification with which we set out. The books of the Bible were written chiefly

by earnest and religious men, devoutly and professed-
ly monotheistic. The writers had no interest in folklore and where they speak of magic and divination,
they speak of it with horror. They did not look for
vestiges of older customs or beliefs and no doubt they
would gladly have disregarded them altogether.
That they did not disregard them was due to the fact
that stories which implied them had already become
sacred, and further to the fact that some of these
customs were recorded by being forbidden. Obviously
if witchcraft was a capital offense, it was because in
caves and hidden recesses witches were now and then
found and punished.

The survival of downright idolatry belongs to the
religious history of the Jews and is not quite within
our chapter. The host of heaven, Ashtoreth and
Molech, the sacred tree and the high place, all these
had been holy for many centuries before the strange
God from Sinai, who delighted in a broken and a
contrite heart rather than in the blood of bullocks,
had ever sent His covenanted tribesmen into ancient
Canaan. But Canaan was very ancient indeed and
the descendant of these tribesmen or of the peoples
they absorbed could scarcely be blamed if he shudder-
ed a little when he passed sites of such old manifesta-
tions. And if to make quite sure he hung a garland
on a hoary terebinth or dropped a honey cake on a
hillock, he would scarcely understand the rage of

zealous prophets when they discovered that he had done so.

There must have been all sorts of men even in the congregation of the Lord, both those whose every movement was guarded by tremulous propitiation of evil eyes and unseen forces, who thought of the Lord of Heaven and Earth as scarcely more than an additional spirit to be placated; and those whose zeal for the Lord brooked nothing that was not explicitly sanctioned by Him. The average man fell in between these two extremes. He did not in later days imitate Micah of Mount Ephraim who had a house of gods and made molten images and eagerly sought the favor of the Lord by taking a Levite into his family. Nor yet had he the stern and ruthless zeal of Jehonadab the son of Rechab to whom Baal worship was a capital crime not unfittingly punished by extermination of the offenders.

CHAPTER XIII

FESTIVALS AND RECREATIONS

To the great majority of the ancient Jews life was toil diversified by festivals in which there was a complete cessation of work. It is an almost universal custom to break up labor by such festivals and the nations surrounding the Jews had many, some coming at regular intervals and some to celebrate special occasions. But the Jews, as far back as we have any knowledge of them, had a practice peculiar to themselves, and that was to make every seventh day a festival. This Sabbath observance, together with their abstention from pork, was almost the first thing noted of the Jews by their neighbors, and it was the fact about them that remained the most generally known. We may add that the Sabbath was far from commending itself to other nations as an institution. A great many thought of it as an example of excessive superstition and others treated it as an absurd self-indulgence. It was inevitable that to external observers the Jews should seem to have too many festivals, when besides the usual ones they had fifty-two additional every year.

Into the origin of the Sabbath and its essential significance we need fortunately not inquire. It has been made the subject of learned quarrels which at the present time have abated a great deal in their intensity. Whatever a Sabbath may have been thousands of years before there were any Jews, the Jewish Sabbath was never a period of fasting and mortification, except possibly to a few zealous sectarians of the Dispersion in Rome and elsewhere. It was, like all other feasts, to be celebrated with sacrifice and it placed especial emphasis on the abandonment of ordinary business, but, in the words of the great poet and prophet whom we call the Second Isaiah, it was also to be "called a delight", to be a source of pleasure even more than ordinary festivals.

These other festivals were frequent; every new moon brought one; the two great seasonal changes were marked by important and ancient feasts; and there were more of varied origin and solemnity. The chief purpose of all of them was religious. They were seasons that belonged to God and in which some visible demonstration must be given of the devotion of the people of the Lord to their sovereign.

It is highly probable that the Hebrew word for festival, *hag*, originally denoted a religious procession or better, a processional dance. Historians of religions tell us that such a dance constitutes the primitive form of worship almost everywhere. We know how it persisted as an element of the cult throughout the ancient world. The *hag* was, in primitive times, music, dance and song simultaneously performed and no one of these elements as it slowly differentiated itself from the mass ever quite lost for the Jews the religious purpose for which it had been devised.

The differentiation had of course taken place long before biblical society assumes a clear and definite form in our eyes. Music, poetry and dancing had then become secular to some extent; they never became so completely secular as they are today. The connection remained longest between dancing and religion and was indeed never broken. Such dancing as our modern dancing of men and women together was unthinkable. When a dance is mentioned it is that of priests leaping about an altar, David leaping before the Lord as the ark comes into the royal city, the daughters of Shiloh dancing in the vineyards when the Benjamites got themselves wives after the fashion made famous in the Roman story. Or else it is Jephthah's daughter meeting her father with timbrels and dances or the women coming up out of all the cities of Israel, singing and dancing, to greet King Saul. Any occasion of joy is a reason for dancing. The marauding Amalekites drink and dance and roll on the ground after they have sacked Ziklag and are still so engaged when David takes bloody vengeance upon them. In fact joy and dancing are practically synonymous terms, since bodily movement has always been a natural and immediate form of expressing emotion.

But it must be apparent that such dancing had none of the organized or systematic form that Greek choral dances later assumed or that modern dancing now possesses. It was an outlet of exuberant feeling, which no doubt quickly fell into some natural rhythm, but the rhythm remained essentially formless. It must have seemed a rude leaping into the air to the cultivated Hellenists in the time of Ben Sira and the Maccabees. Hellenists indeed had dances of their own, provided for them principally by foreign female slaves, dances which were much finer in artistic performance than anything their ancestors could have furnished. But the dangers of this Greek gift are as apparent to us as they were to the sterner moralists of that day. Ben Sira has one briefly disdainful reference and says no more about them. It is small wonder that to him and his fellows dancing of this kind was an additional proof of the evil character of the gods in whose service it was learned.

The other art which never wholly disengaged itself from its early connection with religion was music. We have seen that the exercise of music as a distinct profession was, according to tradition, as old as the oldest handiwork. But there was an even older music than Jubal's harp, the chants or ejaculations uttered in the dance, to which the measures were beaten by cymbals or drums. When music became relatively independent the essential character was still obviously rhythm. Melody played a subordinate part and harmony was virtually unknown.

Melody of course existed. Perhaps we should find little beauty in an ancient Hebrew strain, at any rate until our ears became accustomed to the fact that a different scale from our own was being employed. Apparently the range was smaller, so that the songs would seem somewhat monotonous. Yet definite melodies were obviously known. Several of the Psalms have in their titles such phrases as "After the Hind of the Dawn", "The Dove of the Distant Terebinth", "Destroy Not". It is generally assumed—and no other theory has even plausibility—that these were titles of well-known songs and that the Psalms in question were to be sung to the melodies of those songs. In that case the melodies must have been recognizable strains, something more than mere rhythmic beats between which notes could rise and fall more or less at random.

But in two other important respects ancient Hebrew music was different from ours. An instrument was never played by itself, as violin and piano are now played, but always together with singing or dancing. Yet there was a practice which might easily have grown into solo instrumental performance. Between stanzas, or at other breaks in the song or the dance, it was quite common to execute a sort of free fantasia on whatever instrument was used. The most plausible explanation of the strange word *Selah*, which occurs so often in the Psalms, is that it indicated where these instrumental passages were to come. But this was as far as the development went, and lyres and flutes were generally sounded only to emphasize the notes of a song, or to fill out pauses between notes. There was no real accompaniment as we understand it.

It is this fact which constitutes the second important respect in which biblical music differed from that of modern times. Accompaniments today consist of chords which are struck at the same time as the notes of a melody and harmonize with them. That is also what is done when several instruments play together in quartets or in larger groups. The instruments are played in harmony—a style of music we call polyphonic. Nothing of the kind took place in ancient times. Instruments often played together but they played in unison. A modern orchestra would have been unthinkable and, certainly at first, insufferable to an ancient musician.

We can form a fairly clear picture of what most of the instruments were like. From strictly Jewish pictures we have the six and three string lyre and the straight bronze trumpets of Bar Kokeba's coins, as well as the trumpets on the Arch of Titus. These, to be sure, are later than the period we are considering, but it is highly probable that Jewish instruments closely resembled those of Egypt and Assyria, and since pictures of Assyrian and Egyptian instruments are commonly found on the monuments, we can see not only what they looked like but how they were played.

The Jews had drums and cymbals, harps and lutes, trumpets and flutes, and nearly all the instruments fall into one of these types. The most difficult to play seem to have been the various kinds of flutes or pipes. Skill in playing these was found principally among the the professional musicians belonging to the Temple guilds. There were other guilds which consisted of performers on the harp and cymbals as well as guild singers. Yet it is certain that in no case was musical competence wholly confined to the guilds. A certain familiarity with timbrel and psaltery was wide-spread, and a great many young men who did not belong to the guilds at all learned harp-playing as a personal accomplishment. Cymbals and drums seem to have been played after a fashion by almost anyone. There is the outstanding instance of David, who was a "cunning player on the harp", but the very circumstances of his selection indicate that David's talent, while not unique, was unusual. It may be said that some rudimentary skill in stringed instruments was quite common, but that extraordinary capacity like David's was both rare and highly appreciated.

To play music and to hear music were the most general and typical of diversions. When Job describes the undeserved felicity of the wicked, he mentions as their only pleasures beyond the pride of wealth and power that "they take the timbrel and harp and rejoice at the sound of the organ." If we are to take this literally, most people played the drum and lyre type of instruments themselves, but where instruments like flutes and fifes were concerned, they were rather auditors than performers. Under all circumstances, the passage makes clear that the one art which had the broadest and strongest appeal was the art of music.

Delight in music could be felt, and as Job says, frequently was felt, even by the wicked. There must have been other pleasures common to good men and bad, but the chief mark of the wicked was a certain kind of arrogant ignorance. They were "fools". They said to God: "Depart from us for we desire not the knowledge of Thy ways." If men were virtuous as well as wealthy, the knowledge of the ways of God would be in itself the source of their chief delight, and it would be the form in which the most sophisticated of the arts would present itself.

Literature, to the Jew, in so far as it was something to be enjoyed and not a series of practical memoranda, was always poetry, and poetry was always chant. But the subject matter of this poetry covered much more than the topics which are today poetically treated. History in the form of heroic legends, ethics in the form of moral tales, science in the guise of myths, imaginative narratives taking any and all of these forms, make up a large part of our Bible, although they constituted only a fraction of the poetical literature of the Jews. It is evident that just as music and dance were largely religious in direct application and intention, so also was poetry. Its chief topic was the ways of God: the human activities which it recited were done in the honor of God and the events and facts of the universe it described were God's wondrous handiwork.

But there was also a secular poetry, and, as has been the case from time immemorial, the burden of it was love. Psalm 45, the Song of Loves, is a royal marriage song. The famous Song of Songs is a series of love lyrics of a high quality of beauty, but it is a very human beauty. The name of God does not occur in it, and only a curious determination to call it an allegory, a determination that the Song itself stubbornly resists, caused it to become a part of a sacred canon. There can be no doubt that if our Bible had not so definitely been a religious anthology, such poetry would have been much more fully represented than it actually is.

Whether or not Hebrew poetry had meter we simply do not know. None of the many attempts to discover meter in it have been successful. But it possessed an obvious form which consisted of parallelism, a device whereby the second phrase or clause repeated or supplemented or emphasized the first. One example must suffice, the famous Psalm 114,

"When Israel went out of Egypt,
the house of Jacob from a people of strange language;
Judah became his sanctuary,
and Israel his dominion."

This parallelism was capable of considerable variation and made the rhythmic character of the form thoroughly apparent. But quite apart from matters of form Hebrew poetry and prose are notably different in thought and diction, a difference that is as evident in the translation as in the original.

The enjoyment of poetry was not limited to those who could read and write. Poems were composed long before writing was known and very probably songs were chanted in the public squares. In later times most social gatherings were the occasions of public recitation. But the growth of a literate class made possible the development of a formal and sophisticated literature which only trained minds could really enjoy. Learned men wrote for other learned men and neither sought nor desired a large popular appreciation. The one form of this literature that has come down to us is that of Wisdom, to which such frequent reference has been made, a type that corresponded roughly to the Rhetoric and Philosophy of Greek and Roman society. It may be that at first this was the special possession of a leisured class, men, that is, for whom freedom from toil was not the exceptional privilege of Sabbaths and feasts but the usual condition of their lives. Yet books soon became sufficiently common to make literary avocations possible for men whose ordinary pursuits were toilsome enough, and it is not likely that all this activity was directed to the single end of expounding and illustrating the sacred law.

For there was obviously a poetry completely divorced from religion, a poetry of love and wine, invectives against personal foes, narratives without edifying content, and it is probable that this poetry had artistic qualities of a high order. Most of it, however, has disappeared as far as it was written in Hebrew or Aramaic. The considerable fragments of a secular literature in Greek are late and are plainly the literature of a small class which sought its models outside of the national life.

One conspicuous literary type seems to be wholly lacking, and that is drama. Not far from Palestine on the confines of the tiny land of Attica a dramatic form developed which has dominated the Western world for more than two thousand years. This took place, however, after the highest achievements of Hebrew literary genius had been reached, and the later Jews could not have used the form of the Attic drama without conscious imitation. To such imitation the special character of the Greek play as a heathen ritual formed a powerful obstacle.

Of course a national drama might have developed, as it did among the Hindus, or the Chinese, with or without stimulation from external sources. A dramatic character is almost inherent in ritual and in old narrative poetry. But if tentative steps were taken in that direction they did not go far. The book of Job is so like a drama that a great deal of ingenuity has been expended to prove that it was literally meant to be one, yet the similarity of Job to a play is casual and not essential. Long before the external conditions were created which might have resulted in a real drama, the Jews came into contact with the finest examples this form has ever taken, the perfected Attic tragedy, and it happened to become for them one of the outstanding types of the foreign influences that were most to be repudiated.

Another sort of recreation as hateful to the pious opponents of Hellenism as the Abomination of Desolation itself is mentioned in Second Maccabees. "Now such was the height of Greek fashions and the increase of heathenish manners, that the priests hastened to be partakers of the unlawful allowance in the place of exercise after the game of Discus called them forth." Art may have been the preoccupation or the devoted interest of many Greeks but athletic sports were the delight of nearly all of them. If the author of Second Maccabees is to be believed, the Jews thought such sports essentially heathenish. Yet in all probability it was the place where they were carried on rather than the sports themselves that was really objectionable. We remember two passages of the Bible that have almost the character of proverbs: "The race is not to the swift," and "Rejoiceth as a strong man to run a race." Surely such reference to foot-racing is unintelligible unless the practice of racing was common and gave pleasure. There is an allusion to ball-playing in Isaiah, but it is quite isolated and the ancient Greek translations of the Bible have an altogether different rendering of the passage.

Other sports to which direct and indirect references are made belong to the special class of military exercises. Young soldiers became strong and adroit by wrestling, by throwing the javelin and by archery. It may be that running really belonged here, since we are still in the stage of single combats and we must recall again that Asahel, the son of Zeruiah, "light of foot as a wild roe", was an older contemporary of the swift-footed Achilles. These exercises were therefore not so much sports in which all men shared as they were part of the training for a definite occupation.

That they were competitive was almost inevitable. And the competition must often have taken the form of mock combats. But trials of strength with sword and spear are apt to become cruelly real combats. The "playing" which was a sort of tournament seems to have been indistinguishable from the ancient practice of having as prelude to battle a fight between chosen champions from either side. "Let the young men now arise and play before us," said Abner to Joab. A little later we read the result. "And they caught every one his fellow by the head and thrust his sword in his fellow's side; so they fell down together." This type of "playing" was bound often to have such an end whether it was between rival forces at war or between rivals in times of peace. It was reserved for Roman society to make bloody combats an ordinary spectacle; the gladiatorial arena never gained favor in any part of the Orient.

The elements of chance and danger which gave a zest to these sports made a sport of what was originally an important occupation, that of hunting. In the East particularly, hunting had long been the diversion of kings. Great hunting grounds formed the chief part of the pleasure parks of Oriental monarchs. And what the kings did, the rich and the nobles did on a smaller scale. Yet among the Jews not even the most luxurious and the most heathenish of their kings are credited with much interest in hunting. Herod seems to have been the first to indulge in the pastime. Tradition stigmatized the hunter Esau as rude and barbarous in comparison with his brother and the tradition maintained itself through much later times. Yet hunting is mentioned in the Bible and not infrequently. The principal game animals were harts and antelopes and the principal game birds were partridges. But like fishing this was carried on for a strictly practical purpose. It never became a form of amusement any more than the killing of wild beasts was thought of otherwise than as a necessary measure of protection.

We must suppose that the leisure hours of even rich men were few, else other diversions than these relatively simple ones would have been devised. A world that had no theaters, no games of skill or chance, no foreign travel, no social dances and no athletic sports except for young men or soldiers in training, will doubtless seem bleak enough to our modern eyes. And it is doubtful whether we should think it was much compensation to have music, literature or the study of Wisdom—all three with a strong religious coloring—offered to us. Yet the better sort of man in biblical times seems to have found this occupation of leisure ample and satisfying. What the worse sort did is less explicitly told but can be conjectured. The proportion of vicious to virtuous men was probably not very different from that which prevails today but virtuous men were more easily recognized than they are now by the uses to which they put their leisure hours.

CHAPTER XIV

THE BEASTS OF THE FIELD

THE inhabitants of an ancient city were men and gods. To these must be added, if we wish to have the picture complete, the beasts that perish.

Our own lives would be incompletely described if domestic animals were left out—horses and dogs and cats, parrots and fowls and pigeons. Between these brute creatures and their masters there has grown up a close communion and it expresses itself in emotional forms only a little less important and intense than those which are found between man and man. There is an animal environment as well as a human one.

We no longer reckon seriously with one part of the animal environment which was very close to the ancient Palestinians. The country was not so settled even in its most prosperous days that the jungle lay wholly beyond the range of ordinary experience. Poisonous snakes, while few, were occasionally met with and were greatly dreaded. But the large noxious carnivora were common enough to have enormously impressed men's imagination. A bear robbed of her whelps is the standing type of fury and the lion the constant symbol of courage and strength. These figures might of course have been kept alive by poetical tradition, as in our own speech, long after the animals had practically disappeared; but apparently among the Jews an attack by a lion or a bear on a traveller or sheepfold was a real and present peril. David earned his first repute by killing both these brutes. One of his men-at-arms, Benaiah, became famous for slaying a lion in a pit. The cry, "A lion is in the way", was a not infrequent warning of danger.

A little less familiar, but still known to those who had been down to Egypt or up to Naharaim were three other animals of which the Hebrew names were *reëm*, *behemoth*, and *leviathan*. *Reëm* has been rendered "unicorn" by romantic translators. It designated perhaps some kind of large antelope. *Behemoth* and *leviathan* may have been the hippopotamus and the crocodile or the whale. But even these animals soon became pictures in men's minds and readily grew into the fanciful beasts mediaeval commentators made of them.

The existence of still stranger animals in outlying parts of the world was likewise known to the Jews. Travellers' tales and foreign intercourse brought news of creatures that lived on in popular fancy—apes and elephants and peacocks and the like—but they made little real impression and later poetry and legend use them only slightly.

In its relation to the jungle, Hebrew life while unlike our own was not very different from that of other ancient communities. But in another respect it contrasted with Greek or Roman life almost as much as with our own. The Greeks and Romans lived with domestic animals almost as we do. With the exception of the cat, which came into Europe in comparatively modern times, they saw in their houses and on their streets about the same animal figures that we now see. They too knew and valued the dog to an extent altogether out of proportion to the use they made of him; the horse was a constant companion and a familiar object; barnyard fowls were common and the ludicrous grandeur of the cock, his reputed function as the herald of the dawn, gave him a real hold on popular affection.

The Jews knew practically nothing of all this. The dog to them was an abhorred beast, wandering throughout every city, tolerated as a scavenger and detested as being filthy, cowardly and treacherous. Of any personal association with him, of any attempt to make individual bond between one dog and one master, a Jew would not have dreamed. The legend of Odysseus' favorite dog, Argus, would have been an impossible tale in a Hebrew setting. Even in the oldest and rudest stories of the desert and of the early raids on Canaan there is no tale in which the dog is mentioned otherwise than as a symbol of uncleanness and evil. It is true that one of the famous heroes of the invasion was called "Caleb" or "Dog", and his descendants became an important clan under the ill-favored designation. Still the name stands wholly alone and we are not altogether certain of its meaning.

Nowhere in all Hebrew literature is the dog referred to with a suggestion of kindliness, except in the story of Tobit, an apocryphal book of the first or second century. To call a person a dog was an insult far more outrageous than to hurl any other epithet at him.

The horse too was absent from the ordinary life of biblical men, but for a different reason. He was the animal of war. The early kings possessed horses in direct proportion to the strength of their military establishments. In the great empires to the south and north, in Egypt and Assyria, the mark of their overwhelming strength was the number of their horses. Rab Shakeh, the Assyrian captain, tauntingly challenges Hezekiah of Judah by offering him two thousand horses if he can find men in his army to mount them. The splendid picture of a horse in Job is drawn by an expert, but it is the picture of a war horse.

The ordinary animal of conveyance was the ass, of which there were many varieties. For the nobles and the powerful there were white asses and, in later times, mules. These beasts had nothing ridiculous or contemptible about them in the eyes of the Jews. They symbolized neither stupidity nor uncomplaining endurance. The term "ass" is never used as an epithet of derision, and the possession of many asses is as evident a mark of great wealth as that of horses would have been to an Athenian. When Zechariah tells us of the Messiah who will come riding upon an ass it is not meant as a mark of humility but as a symbol of the reign of peace. Wars, we remember, would cease forever in the Messianic age and the ass was as emphatically the beast of peace as the horse was of war.

The absence of the horse and the dog from our picture of every-day life would itself make a sharp external contrast between our society and that of the Bible. The contrast is deepened by the presence in the city as in the country of the camel, that strange, ungainly beast which seems to us peculiarly fitted for the menageries in which we generally see him. Camels served every purpose except that of food. Their milk was drunk, their hair used as wool, they were yoked to carts or wagons and were particularly the riding animals for long distances. In that respect the desert and the settled land showed a difference only in degree. Camels were indispensable to the nomads and formed the chief item in the enumeration of the wealth of the wild tribes. In Palestine they were an important element, but only one among many, in the social economy. No reference need be made here to animals like sheep and cattle, the purpose of whose existence seemed exhausted in the use man made of them. If barnyard fowls were known, they were similarly thought of solely as food.

We might be inclined to say from all this that the Hebrew used domestic animals but made no pets of them. But that can hardly be true in the unqualified form in which it is often stated. There is the parable which Nathan told to David of the poor man who had "nothing save one little ewe lamb which he had brought and nourished up; and it grew up together with him and with his children; it did eat of his own meat and drank of his own cup and lay in his bosom and was to him as a daughter." It is the only mention we have of such an incident but it cannot have been a unique case. Young girls seem to have played with birds by attaching a string to their legs, or by teaching them to come at call. At any rate we may guess this from the passage in Job in which Job is asked, "Wilt thou play with him (the leviathan) as with a bird: wilt thou bind him for thy maidens?" The playing of kids and lambs is often mentioned in poetry as a symbol of joy. Men took real pleasure in watching them and the emotions excited must have been in some measure transferred to the animals themselves. And finally there is the phrase in the strangely abrupt close of the Book of Jonah which seems to include the cattle under those who enjoyed divine protection.

All these are but hints and we should gladly welcome more express statements that showed the existence of real feeling in the matter. Yet we must remember that there is also no evidence of any ill-treatment of beasts, not even of dogs. If the proverb is true that a merciful man is merciful to his beast, it may be remembered that the ancient Hebrews by the testimony of their enemies were merciful men.

Humanitarian legislature in our day forbids cruelty to animals. It is of very recent origin. Until the middle of the nineteenth century, cruelty to beasts in any form was morally reprehensible in certain very limited groups but was nowhere illegal. Among the Jews, however, certain forms of ill-treatment of animals were illegal as well as immoral. It was, for example, forbidden to muzzle an ox while he trod the corn or to yoke an ox and an ass together to the plough. Other motives, besides those of kindliness, may have played a part in determining these rules, but ancient and modern commentators have agreed in seeing in these prohibitions a desire to spare the animals a needless and purposeless hardship.

There are two other passages in the Pentateuch which have often been cited as indicating humanitarian motives in ancient Hebrew legislation. They are the prohibitions against taking a brooding bird and against seething a kid in its mother's milk. The Alexandrian philosopher Philo took them to be proofs of almost excessive humaneness in the law of Moses and he has been followed by many modern commentators. It is possible that he was right in regard to the brooding bird, but as far as the kid is concerned, it seems more likely that the seething was prohibited because it formed part of a heathen ritual and was therefore an abomination.

Similarly we can draw no intelligent inferences from the list of animals which were allowed and those which were forbidden for food. These prohibitions made a sharp severance between Jews and non-Jews, but they belong to the wide-spread class of observances known as food taboos and give us little help in determining what the popular attitude toward these animals was. At first there was no abhorrence of swine and none of hares, both of which were forbidden and were very common. Certainly there was no abhorrence of asses and camels and horses, which were also forbidden as food. Deer, which were not fit for sacrifice, were not unclean for food. Goats seemed the embodiments of evil spirits but were both sacrificed and eaten.

It is highly probable that the influences which created the food taboos were of varied origin. Our available information does not suffice to explain them. Nor can we now discover the real significance of the fact that some few biblical personages used as personal names the names of animals. Those who find in this fact indications of an ancient totemism may remember that names like Lion, Bear, Wolf, excessively rare among ancient Jews, became extremely common among mediaeval Jews and their modern descendants.

CONCLUSION

In bringing our brief survey of an ancient society to an end it will be well to bear in mind the cautions with which we began. The people with whom we have been dealing seem often extraordinarily like ourselves. That is due not to a real or imagined identity of blood but to the fact that the human mind has in the last thirty-two centuries suffered practically no change. What has changed enormously is the concrete environment. If in some respects the Israelite seems to act like a strange unaccountable person it is due to the latter cause. He had to deal with different facts and his habitual conduct in regard to them reacted upon himself.

But there is no chasm between biblical men and ourselves—none, that is, which we cannot bridge with a little imagination. We need merely avoid attributing to their world the concrete framework which we see about us in ours. We must remember that their habits were as different from ours as their clothing. But if this allowance be made, we can safely impute to them the same emotions, the same joys and fears, as those we have; and we certainly have no reason for supposing that the average of intelligence among them was one whit lower than our own.

Perhaps the greatest barrier to an understanding of how men lived at that time has been that the record of their activities has become a sacred book; but it must be evident that whatever sacredness this book possesses must depend on other elements than the account it gives or implies of the life of the people. The great names of the biblical story and the lesser names that accompany them lose nothing, it seems to me, if we forget for a moment their function as exemplars of conduct, and remember only their essential humanity.

INDEX